Love Letters 1909:

A Long Distance Romance
Through the Mail

Edited and Compiled by

Cherilyn Clough

ISBN: 978-0-9960332-0-6

Table Rock Press

Dedicated to my Mom, Elaine, who adored Estella,
and to Estella, who made us both feel loved.

This is a true story.
The letters you are about to read
have been minimally edited
with respect to content and are not fiction,
but a real life conversation.

Table of Contents

Children of a New Century

Estella is a modern girl who prefers living in town instead of the family farm. She enjoys her job as a candy maker and has a lively social life, but she still spends the occasional evening alone with her black cat. Most of her friends are already married, but Estella is holding out for the right man. When she mails a postcard to an old friend, she hopes for a quick reply. She never dreams it will reach a stranger with the same name.

Edwin is a machinist who has little time to look for a wife. Since the death of his father, he has been taking care of his mother and sisters. He spends his evenings writing marches and practicing maneuvers for the Michigan National Guard. He is one of the best marksmen in the state—a fact his mother finds ironic since he can't kill a chicken for dinner. When the postcard arrives addressed to a Mr. Edwin Ellis, he realizes it was intended for someone else, but he can't resist the opportunity to answer it.

Hidden in a trunk for over a century, these letters have been patiently waiting to tell their story. What you are about to read is not fiction, but a real life conversation between strangers who have never met. Each letter has been carefully preserved with minimal editing.

Edwin and Estella are children of a new century. The horse and buggy world of their childhood is quickly disappearing and driving machines are taking over. Their discussions cover many topics from healthcare and employment to religion and politics. Each conversation gives us a glimpse into the Progressive Era.

When they first correspond in 1908, Henry Ford is experimenting with an assembly line for his new-fangled machines and Carl Fisher is about to make his dream come true by creating the Indianapolis Motor Speedway—soon to be known as the Indy 500. Edwin's letters include a descriptive and historical eyewitness account of the third race during opening week.

Kodak is providing a new way to preserve memories. Edwin now carries his own camera with him everywhere he goes—taking pictures of whatever or whomever he chooses.

The world seems to be getting smaller. Explorers are about to conquer both the North and South Poles. A luxurious new ship named the Titanic is being built, which will change the way people view travel across the Atlantic. There are rumors it is unsinkable.

Even the breakfast table is changing. The Kellogg brothers have discovered a way to make a flaked cereal that saves housewives time making breakfast. Estella works for the Kellogg Company in Sanita's Candy Kitchen.

Ragtime Bands are the pop music of the day. Edwin writes his own marches and plays with his militia marching band.

They both have dreams of finding a spouse and starting a family, but they live 70 miles apart. Travel is arduous in a day when people are still using a horse and buggy and roads are scarce even if you have a car. Their best chance of meeting is to take the train, but first they must decide if their relationship is worth the ticket.

For now, their future hangs in the balance. Edwin has a postcard from a girl he has never met. Estella has no idea the wrong man received her card. Was it a twist of fate, or Providence that sent this letter to the wrong address? Will Edwin reveal the truth, or keep the conversation going? Will Estella find his practical joke to be funny?

Edwin's band is practicing a love song while the train carries his response from Grand Rapids to Battle Creek. Estella's heart is beating to its own rhythm as she reaches for the letter because she believes she recognizes the handwriting.

Estella's Male Mix Up

5/11/08
Grand Rapids

Dear Miss Stella,

Your postal was received, but I have not been in Detroit for some time. I am living and working in Grand Rapids and expect to stay put. Work is not very plenty here, but I am one of the favored few who have work.

My address is Edwin Ellis
No. 50 13th St
Grand Rapids, Mich.

I will write more when I hear from you.

Mr. Edwin Ellis,
Grand Rapids, Mich.

****

5/22/08
Battle Creek Mich.

Dear Old Friend,

I was surprised in two ways when I received your letter and card. First, I had my doubts as to whether I would find you and second, because when I did hear from you the letter was so short.

May and I thought it over and came to the conclusion you were married, were we right?

Regardless, we were very glad to hear from you and your whereabouts.

You said you were among the favored few who had work, well I guess we are too, work is scarce everywhere now. We are the only two left out of five girls who worked for Kellogg in the Sanita's Candy Kitchen when I came here last fall.

What are you working at now? May said when she received a letter from you about two years ago you were learning a trade in Detroit. She answered your letter and gave you my address and you never wrote to either of us, why not?

May and I took quite a liking to you because you acted so gentlemanly with us when we were with you on the farm and in Chicago.

I can never forget you — you should always remember you have a cozy corner in our hearts. I remember the sad parting at the boat when we left you standing on the dock. I think you must have a faint recollection of it, haven't you?

May says I should tell you hello for her. She says I am telling you all the news so there isn't much left for her to write. We are not working this afternoon and May says she is lonesome so she is going down to see her sister Lulu Parsons. You remember her.

May and I work together and room together — you know we were always quite chummy. I got tired of staying on the farm and you remember the fellow I was going with when you saw me? Well he and I fell out last winter and consequently I am still single and not in much of a hurry to change that.

My sister Grace Foote and husband live on a farm close to my folks in Indiana. They have a very sweet little girl.

While May is gone to see her sister and I am all alone, I sure wish you were here to have a good old chat. Good old times we had in the berry patch, didn't we? Times I will never forget. Remember our shanty? How the floor almost caved in with us?

Wonder where funny-graph is now? Poor boy, I certainly felt sorry for him. And George, he was a good boy, but he was always rather quiet and backward.

Well, I will close for now, but I expect to get a long newsy answer to this letter. Write soon and tell me all about yourself.

I remain yours with best respects,

Miss Estella Mellinger

Edwin's Confession

May 28, 1908
Grand Rapids, Mich.

Dear Miss Stella,

Your letter was received and now, if you will listen for a few moments, I will spring a little surprise on you — trusting that you will pardon me for doing so.

My name is Edwin Ellis, but evidently not the one you have in mind. The only other Edwin Ellis in this city that I know of is our Mayor George E. Ellis whose middle name is Edwin. Knowing that your card could not be meant for him, I decided to answer it myself.

By odd coincidence, I have been in both Detroit and Chicago. I worked in Chicago for three years. My stay in Detroit was short however. I was selected as one of a team of four who represented our company for the local battalion of the Michigan National Guard for the state shoot.

I am curious to hear more about this namesake of mine. I dare say from the remarks in your letter that I need not be ashamed of him as a namesake.

Now I think I have written all I ought to for this time and should you see fit to make reply, I will be pleased to answer it in a more congenial and interesting way.

Trusting I have made things clear and you will pardon me for taking this liberty, I remain very respectfully,

Edwin Ellis
June 20, 1908
Battle Creek, Michigan

Dear Sir,

I received your letter about two weeks ago. Upon opening it, I expected to hear from my old friend, but as you said, you sprung quite a surprise on me. Your writing is just like that of my old friend's handwriting. I have always admired his writing and could never have told the difference in the writing.

I was somewhat surprised at the coolness of the first letter. Not hearing from him for two years, I thought he was probably married — that would account for it. Seeing you are a stranger, I can overlook it. I enjoyed your letter very much.

About three years ago my folks moved to a farm not far from Lafayette, Indiana. I thought I would enjoy country life, but I got very lonely. I was not used to the quiet countryside.

Like most girls, I enjoy working for myself rather than staying at home. I have always enjoyed Battle Creek more than any city I have visited so am here working for the Sanita's candy department.

It is very desirable work for this warm weather as we worked in a room with the temperature about 66 to 70 degrees. We are certainly having some warm weather aren't we?

It seems I have written enough for this time, but I will tell you a little more about your name-sake. We met in a rather queer way. A crowd of us young folks from here went out into the country near Benton Harbor to pick berries. We met several young men there and had some good times — both in the berry patch and in the after work hours. We played ball games under the apple trees and were near the St. Joe River so we could go boat riding.

Just before we left to go to our homes, this Mr. Ellis, another lady and I took a trip to Chicago on the steamer and this is the trip I spoke about. I can only speak well of him although our acquaintance was limited. If you should ever meet him, I would be pleased to have you mention me to him.

I will cut my letter short now and be pleased to hear from you again.

I remain a new acquaintance,

Miss Estella Mellinger

The Last of the Line

Grand Rapids
July 10, 1908

Dear Miss Stella,

Your letter was received some time ago. If you will pardon my negligence, I will endeavor to answer it now.

I have a great curiosity bump and my curiosity still deepens in regard to this namesake of mine since you say his writing resembles mine. I wonder if he is unfortunate enough to look anything like me.

The first Ellis family in this country came from Wales and landed at Plymouth, MA about the middle of the seventeenth century. Every Ellis I have ever met came from that same stock of this original family.

There is one Herbert Ellis whom I would like to find if he is still alive. He is the only male cousin I have bearing the name because he was the only son of his father and I am the only living son of my father both of whom are dead.

His father died while he was quite young. His mother moved away with him and we have never heard from them since. So you see if he is not in existence that makes me the only male descendant of my immediate family bearing the name.

Well this dabbling too far into family affairs is certainly not a very interesting subject to you, so I will change it.

I have never visited Lafayette. As a matter of fact the only time I have ever been to Indiana was when I visited two years ago with the Michigan state troopers. We camped out at Benjamin Harrison for ten days. While there I found the Indiana people to be very hospitable and social.

I was the K Company cook that year and I will tell you of an experience we had with a storm. It happened on our second day in camp. We had just gotten our supper ready and we were about to blow mess call when I looked up and discovered a small cloud had suddenly assumed large, black and threatening proportions.

I covered up our coffee and hustled a large pan of baked beans back into the oven. Then we carried our bread, cookies and other perishable stuff up and into our commissary tent with no time to spare.

Just then the storm struck and it certainly had a lot of amusement at our expense for about an hour. The rain fell down — not in drops, but in lakes. And the wind — well it had all the Michigan winds I ever seen beat by fifty miles. The tent that I and my squad occupied blew down on us. I took to the open air preferring to take my chance in the open rather than get mixed up with a big piece of canvas especially when it was trying to settle such a grievance with such a wind as that.

Just then the tent next to me collapsed and fell down. What appeared to be numerous bumps under the wet canvass suddenly came to life and after a good bit of pawing and squirming came crawling from under the tent taking the form of wet soldier boys. The language that filled the air between the raindrops and lakes would have been very unwholesome in the presence of a Sunday School Teacher.

One half of the tents on the grounds were blown down and a great many of the companies lost their supper that night, but as soon as the storm was over we resurrected our baked beans and coffee and our boys had a good warm supper.

The next day resembled a general wash day. Every bit of string and rope about the camp was strung up and filled full of wet clothes to dry. Others were stretched out on the ground. It was truly a bit of real soldier's life. We expect to camp at the same place this year.

I think you would be pleased with a visit to Grand Rapids and if you should ever do so, I would be pleased to meet my namesake's old friend.

Well my letter is assuming a somewhat tiresome length as you can verify by the writing so I will draw to a close hoping to receive an early reply.

I remain yours very truly,

Edwin Ellis

****

Edwin's concerns about being the end of the line are justified. His father has passed on and he is the ninth generation in a line of Ellis's who have traced their lineage back to Plymouth Rock.

His mother came from the White family who also date their tree back to the same time and the same state. Her family claims to be descended from Peregrine White, who was the first child born into the New World on the Mayflower as it docked just off of Cape Cod. But records are scanty and no one knows for sure. If this is a rumor, it is not a new one because three generations into the new world we find his family giving their son the middle name of Peregrine.

With so few people in Massachusetts at the time, It's a wonder an Ellis did not marry a White sooner. Edwin was a man whose parents and grandparents took obvious pride in tracing their family roots to the first families in the New World, and he appears to feel pressure to not be the last of the line.

His last letter was dated July 10th. The next letter we find is dated October 4th. Were there other letters that were lost? Notice Edwin is now addressing Estella in a more formal tone. Perhaps he thought it wise to give her some time to get used to the idea of someone new. Maybe he wanted to make sure she liked him for more than just his good name. Oh, wait a minute... it appears Estella has stopped writing.

****

Oct. 4, 1908
Grand Rapids, Mich.

Dear Miss Mellinger,

In the early part of August I received a letter from you and answered shortly after. At the same time I sent you some postcard views of Grand Rapids, but to this date I have never received any reply. So I will take the liberty to write once more — trusting you will pardon me for doing so.

Now Miss Mellinger, please do not think me over persistent. I would not under any condition force attention upon anyone, but I have always had a great dread of mistakes and misunderstandings. So if you have received my letter and do not care to write anymore, it would be but a short task to you and I assure you a favor to me, if you will drop me a few lines stating as much. Then there would be no misgivings on my part as to whether or not my letters have reached you.

I have some postcard photographs I took while encamped with the state troopers at Indianapolis last week, which I might send if I was sure they were going to reach you.

Trusting you will receive this letter with the good spirit of which it was sent.

I remain,

Very respectfully,

Edwin Ellis

P.S. I have not yet found anything of your friend and my namesake. His name does not appear in this year's city directory.

****

For now, we can hear Edwin sigh as he walks to the post office. Does Estella think he is too pushy? Has she discovered her long lost friend? Or has her family discouraged her from writing to a man she has never met? I guess we'll have to let her choices play out until we discover the answer.

True Believer

Oct. 8, 1908
Grand Rapids, Mich.

Miss Estella Mellinger

Dear Friend,

I was both surprised and pleased when I came home from work last evening and found your letter. I had just mailed a letter to you that morning.

I had quite a nice time camping in Indiana. Of course our work was somewhat hard and strenuous, but that was to be expected. They put us through quite a severe course of military maneuvers under the supervision of U. S. Army officers.

Our forenoons were usually confined to field tactics in the large open field. The afternoons were a test of mimic warfare — as if we were in actual war with the expectation that blank ammunition would be used instead of service.

There were three regiments from Michigan, one from Wisconsin and one from Kentucky beside two regiments of U. S. Army regulars making it in all about five thousand troops. We were divided into what they called the blues and the browns. The blues wore shirts without the blouses while the brown wore the brown khaki blouse. One side would be sent out to occupy a position somewhere in the surrounding country. The other side, without knowing where their opponents were, would be sent out to find them and route them from their position if they could.

There are mounted army officers with white bands around their arms or hat called referees. They are to judge who is the winning side. It sounds quite realistic when three or four thousand troops get into action with blank ammunition.

One of the strictest rules is to keep under cover as much as possible. Any small or large detachment of men who are caught by the referees unnecessarily exposing themselves to the enemy's fire are quickly ruled out and considered captured.

When we reached Indiana on the 21st of September, they had not had any rain for forty-one days. Everything was terribly dry and parched. Most of the rivers and creeks were completely dry and you can imagine what the roads were. The soldiers suffered more from the heat and dust than anything else.

On the night of Sunday the 27th, it rained most of the night and the remaining three days were much better.

****

The rest of this letter is missing as is the letter from Estella that he refers to in the beginning. I suppose they never dreamed we would be reading them and wondering what happened to the missing parts, so we will forgive them for this and read on.

****

Oct. 19, 1908
Grand Rapids, Mich.

Miss Estella Mellinger

Dear Friend,

I was somewhat pleased last Monday evening when I returned from my work and found your letter waiting for me. My sister laughed at me because I read your letter at the supper table before I ate. She said I must have relished your letter better than I did my supper.

I also received that box of candy and say, it is the nicest and most palatable candy I have ever tasted and I am quite a candy eater. It does not have that intense sweet which is so predominant in other candies which are palatable for a short time and soon make one feel as though they have had plenty and sometimes a little bit more than plenty.

I thank you ever so much for it and I scarcely know how to retaliate. However I will send you some photographs of the camp happenings. I do not have them all made yet, but they will be forthcoming soon. And say Miss Mellinger, while we are speaking about pictures, let me make a suggestion. If you care to, I will be pleased to exchange photos. If you will send me a photo of yourself, I will do likewise by return mail.

You asked me if I belong to any church. I was raised Baptist and am now a member of the Scribner Street Baptist Church of this city, although I am not much of a credit. I, like you, am a strong believer. There are times when my belief has been a source of great comfort and consolation to me.

While I am a believer, I am not a narrow minded fanatic. Neither do I believe in a Christianity so broad that it will allow one to go to church on their Sabbath day and listen to the teachings of the Bible, then go home and live entirely apart from it the rest of the week. I am a little careless sometimes, but I am always trying to do better.

Grand Rapids has about 110,000 people. Yes, we have about the highest class of theatrical talent come through here. I do not go to the theater often. I have been twice in the last year — although I do like to take in the Grand Operas when they come. They are much different and more elaborate than the theatrical plays. The Savage Grand Opera Co. has an orchestra of its own with forty instruments. Everything is sung or played. Not a word is spoken outside of their singing — sometimes in single parts, sometimes in chorus. The whole play is in music.

Although I am fond of music, I am not much of a player myself. We have a piano and my sister plays some. I make a very few noises — which from a distance, might at the first impulse be mistaken for music. But upon closer inspection, would be found to be a series of harmonious discords which might be better appreciated at a distance — if the distance were far enough.

However, I do have some pieces of my own composition which I have written off as a pastime. They are in the shape of marches and two steps and other people say nice is the most I can say for them. I have not as of yet had any of them published.

At different times I have played in bands. I usually play first B flat cornet. We also have an orchestra in the battalion here.

My curiosity still deepens in regards to this namesake of mine. I should really like to find him.

Well, I shall ask you to excuse this uninteresting letter this time and I will try and do better next time.

Hoping to hear from you soon,

I remain as ever your friend,

Edwin

P.S. Will send you postcards someday next week. Don't forget to think over the photo proposition.

****

Oct. 24, 1908
Battle Creek, Mich.

Dear Friend,

I have just read your letter again and I think I can give you an answer. As I sat here rocking myself this afternoon and listening to the wind howl down through the chimney, I thought of what you said about the music you can make. It seems I must be just at a suitable distance to distinguish those harmonious discords and I really think it seems soothing enough to put me to sleep.

Well Mr. Ellis, you must have a real pleasant home. I think music is a great comfort in a home. Well I guess you can set your music up with the majority. I would like a copy of the pieces you composed. Why don't you have them published?

So your curiosity is still alive concerning your namesake? So is mine, but he has probably died in the last couple of years and we just don't know it.

Yes, Mr. Ellis, I would be pleased to exchange photos with you. You can look for it most any day.

Oct. 25, 1908

Well Mr. Ellis, I failed to finish your letter yesterday so I will try to finish it this evening. This is Sunday evening and all the folks have gone to a stereo-fiction lecture. I am all alone and I tell you I feel rather fearful. It is growing quite cold and windy tonight. I think I will go to bed when I get through writing this letter.

Say, while speaking about the weather, I think it would be a treat to have a little rain once again to put out the fires all over the country, don't you? There was a marsh swept by fire about a half mile from here just a few nights ago. We didn't know about it at the time — although the air was so full of smoke we could scarcely breathe one night last week. Today we went for a walk and were surprised to discover the marsh is all burned black.

I am glad you enjoyed your candy. We make several different kinds of which I sent you my favorite. Some people prefer others. If you should ever come to Battle Creek at any time, I would be pleased to have you call on me.

It is just now eight o'clock, but I am getting cold and sleepy and I think I have made you weary already, so I think I will cease my writing and go to bed.

Looking forward to an early reply and those postcards.

I remain your true friend,

Estella Mellinger

Please overlook mistakes and poor writing for it is simply me.

So there you have it. Two strangers have been sharing their hearts through these letters for six months and now they are getting curious about what the other looks like. They have agreed to exchange pictures, but who will discover what the other looks like first?

Duel of the Missing Photographs

Nov. 1, 1908
Grand Rapids, Mich.

Friend Stella,

Your letter was received. Now, if you have a few moments to listen, I will try to keep you busy for that short length of time. This is Sunday evening and since I did not go to church tonight, I will improve the time by writing to you.

This has been an exceptionally fine day for this time of year. The sun was shining nearly all day. But I almost dread to think of what is to come later when the cold bleak winds begin to howl around the corners of the house and pile up big snow drifts in front of the doors. At such times I sometimes feel a slight inclination to go south to live. However, winter though bleak and cold is not without its charms. As we sit in a warm and comfortable home, we look out of our windows into the beautiful mantle of pure white in which nature has clothed everything. We cannot help but think we are looking out on one of nature's most beautiful works of art.

Then in the evening, we hear the merry laughter and shouts mingled with the silvery jingling of sleigh bells. A sleigh ride party is passing the house on their way to some farmer's house out in the rural district. There they will have a jolly old time such as only a farmer's home can give them. These and many other things break the monotony of the bleak cold winter and lend charms which help to make winter not an altogether unwelcome visitor.

But Stella, did it ever occur to you while sitting in your own home by a warm fireside while the cold blustery winds are howling outside—that somewhere out in these bitter cold elements are hundreds of creatures both human and dumb brutes, who are less fortunate than us? Either by misfortune, or natural consequence they suffer nature's cruelest inflictions and in nearly all cases, due to the misjudgment of mankind.

For the wild beasts in their natural haunts, nature has provided instincts and habits which enable them to care for themselves. But the domestic animals, which the Creator has placed in our care, oftentimes bear untold cruelty and suffering for which man alone is responsible.

How often in passing some of our downtown saloons do we see a team of horses hitched outside without blankets, facing a blustering storm while their driver may be found inside. He is leaning over the bar with a beer glass in his hand or sitting by a table near a warm stove engaged in a game of cards.

One game follows after another until hours have passed by with little thought of the poor dumb brutes waiting outside? The most faithful of man's dumb servants—have they been thought of during these hours of comfort by this driver? At last, he awakes to the fact that it is long past time he was home. He goes out to climb into his sleigh and the poor brutes are driven at a break-neck pace for home.

The same thing may apply to the man who spends his time and money in the saloon while his wife and children are at home suffering for the want of food and warmth. These are a few of the many offsets of the glory and pleasure we find in our beautiful winters.

The treat which you spoke about in the way of rain has come and gone and it certainly must have been a blessing to those who live in the fire district. A forest fire is a rather serious thing and hard to conceive when one has never witnessed it.

A few years ago my folks lived in the north part of the state in a little lumbering town called Echo Lake. A fire broke out one time in the pine slashings adjoining the village. These are dead pine tree tops and underbrush left behind after the trees were cut and they make the most excellent fuel for the fire to work in. The fire was quickly creeping up onto the town when fortunately it began to rain. It seemed almost like an act of Providence.

I'm looking for your photo which has not come yet. You may look for mine most any day. By the way you have dark hair haven't you? Tell me if I am not right? I have sent you a package of photographs which you will have no doubt have received by this time. I will send you some different ones on postals as soon as I get time to finish them.

Well Stella, I guess I kept you company for a few minutes so I will draw to a close for now.

I am hoping to hear from you soon and to receive your photo.

In the meantime I remain as always,

Your friend,

Edwin

P.S. Please excuse mistakes and poor writing as I see they are both plentiful.

Nov. 6, 1908
Battle Creek, Mich.

Dear Friend — I have just a few minutes to write before I go to work.

I was very pleased to get your letter and those pictures you sent — they are real nice. My folks are discussing among themselves as to whether the one picture was you or not. I told them they couldn't prove it by me. I hope to tell better when you send your photo. I am curious to get it, but I guess you will have to wait awhile now for mine.

I had some nice pictures taken a few weeks ago and when I went to get them there was some mistake made and they were not what I wanted. I had paid $1.50 on them and because they were not just what I wanted, I asked him to let me take just three of them and I'd have some more taken. The photographer would not let me have even one unless I took all. So I wouldn't take any, and he kept the $1.50. I suppose he burned up all the pictures rather than let me have even one. So I haven't any pictures now unless I send you a postcard picture. But never mind, I will go someplace else to have them taken.

Feel free to send yours any time now and I will remember you as soon as I get mine again.

So you think my hair is dark, do you? What makes you think so? You can judge when I send you my picture. You aroused my curiosity to wonder what makes you think my hair is dark.

How does the election suit you Mr. Ellis? I suppose we will have better times for a while now, don't you think?

You certainly laid out some very sad pictures in that last letter, but never the less often true. I would like to see the saloons wiped entirely out of our country. I belong to the Michigan Anti-Saloon League and I believe they are doing a good work.

Well, I will have to cut my visit short and go to work.

So bye bye.

Ever your friend,

Estelle

****

It seems like these two people are eager to see what the other looks like, yet rather slow to send their own picture. Ideally one would like to see the other person before showing oneself. Definitely not an issue in today's dating scene.

Edwin is quite the writer. His letter makes me want to move south. I couldn't help but laugh at the picture of this young woman rushing to open the mail and then reading all the bleak midwinter scenes. Perhaps he should have said, "Now if you have a few moments, I will try to depress you for that length of time." What a way to court a woman!

How to Bore a Woman with Politics

Nov. 17, 1908
Grand Rapids,

Friend Stella,

Your letter was received a week ago yesterday and once more I will have to plead guilty in being a little bit negligent in answering. I also received your postcard photo with the one marked with a cross which I take to be you.

It was certainly a small and narrow minded bit of transaction that the photographer played on you. It goes to show how much some people can belittle themselves in their dealings with other people. Yet you may hear this same class of people say "Well, business is business and that's my way." They will put on a bold front and act brave when they have a few cents the best of you, but when the shoe fits on the other foot or when confronted with a few honest suggestions they will whine and cry like a whipped cur.

These are what I call people with a price on themselves. And their price is a small paltry sum with which you buy them when they attempt to cheat you as this man did.

Please do not think I am sarcastic, as you would find if you were better acquainted with me (which you might be someday) this is not the case at all. I am only expressing a few sentiments and placing them where I think they belong. I think you will quite agree with me.

No doubt you have received my photo by this time and I shall look for yours in the meantime. The one you speak of in the package of photographs is of myself taken in front of my tent at camp last fall.

You ask me how the elections suited me. Well, the general election suited me very well with the possible exception of governor and some of the candidates on our local ticket. Grand Rapids is a very strong Republican town; there is also a very strong faction between the saloon and anti-saloon elements — with the saloon element slightly in the lead on this occasion.

I do not think it would have been this way if it were not for the presidential election. A great many people are adverse to splitting their ticket on a presidential election year for fear of making a mistake and having their whole ballot thrown out.

The election of a prosecuting attorney means a great deal for either side. A man by the name of Brown ran on the Republican ticket. He was backed up by the liberal or saloon element. He was opposed by a Democrat named Adolph Ellis who was backed up by the antis. Brown was elected by a five hundred majority whereas the Republican majority in general went from three to four thousand. The antis are gaining every year and it is predicted by some of the liberals themselves that Grand Rapids will go dry in a few years.

Thank you very much for your invitation to call on you and I may avail myself of the opportunity to accept your invitation sometime in the near future. I will let you know beforehand when it will be.

So your curiosity is aroused as to what makes me think your hair is dark? Well, I will tell you sometime, but first you must guess. I doubt if you can. You may make the attempt however.

Well Stella, it is getting rather late and I am somewhat sleepy so I will bid you goodnight.

Hoping to receive an early reply,
I wish to remain

Your friend,

Edwin

****

Nov. 26, 1908
Battle Creek, Mich.

Mr. Edwin Ellis,

Kind friend, I hope you will pardon me for not writing sooner, but I have been between two straights.

The young man whom I am going with here objects to my corresponding to any other young man. Although I have enjoyed your letters very much and will certainly miss their visits, I think it would only be fair to discontinue our correspondence.

I am sorry for a good many reasons, but I know you will agree with me that it is not right to continue if I think anything of the other young man. I was pleased to get your photo and I suppose you now have mine as well.

I also received your two cards yesterday which were very nice. I hope this does not bar out our friendship and if such is the case that you should be in our city or I in yours, I would be pleased to meet you just the same.

Wishing to remain a friend to you,

I am Miss Estelle Mellinger

P.S. Would be pleased to receive an answer.

****

I wonder if Edwin ever swears. This would be the time for it. Being a diligent Christian — it doesn't seem so, but I can imagine him reading Estella's letter this time and asking, "What in the world?"

I also don't know if Estella agreed or disagreed or cares about his political talk, but I've got to wonder if all this political talk might not be causing her to rethink their potential relationship.

Or maybe it's the fact that he thinks he knows her hair color.

Or perhaps it's the way he said she might be "better acquainted" with him someday.

Or maybe she had second thoughts when she saw his picture.

Maybe she feels things are going too fast, so she decided to find a new, safer beau overnight. It must be weird for Edwin — they've been writing for months and this is the first time we've heard of another man.

Never fear dear reader, there will be more letters to come. I guess some people just like to take it slow.

Nobody to Kiss on New Year's Eve

Jan. 5, 1909
Battle Creek, Mich.

Kind Friend,

It has been some time since I last heard from you. I have wondered if you received the card and box of candy I sent you just about Christmastime. But I thought you are probably waiting to get an answer to your letter, so I am going to write you a short letter.

Your last letter touched a rather tender spot in my heart. We are now living in a new year — one year nearer to the end. As you said in your letter, time is short. I don't believe we realize how near the end is, do we? I've been very careless of late, but I am determined to improve the opportunities the Lord gives me — more this year than last year.

My sister has taken an old gentleman friend in. He came to the city with his wife who is taking treatments and while here he was taken sick too. He is sick with typhoid fever, but getting along very well. We all have hopes of him getting well soon. We have a sanitarium nurse and my sister and brother in law are both nurses too, so he has good care. There are many ways we can do good and the Lord will bless us.

I am not trying to flatter you at all, but I will say by the tone of your letters you are a very considerate and thoughtful young man. I do not intend to drop you from my correspondence or list of friends.

I want to get better acquainted with you if the opportunity affords me to in the near future. So if you have not changed your mind and still desire to call on me, you will be welcome if you let me know when you can come.

Don't worry about the other party. Your letter set me to thinking and I am grateful for your friendship to me as needed. I also want you to feel at liberty to be a friend when not needed.

Your little piece of music was very nice and I am still looking for the music you had published. I suppose you had a very pleasant Christmas. I had a nice time and received quite a few nice presents.

Now, you ended your letter by calling yourself a "silent friend." I say you need not be silent unless you particularly care to. I enjoy your letters and cards and would miss them very much if you cease to write.

I will close hoping to receive an early reply and waiting for your opinion.

Yours truly,

Miss Estelle Mellinger

Jan. 10, 1909
Grand Rapids, Mich.

Friend Estella,

Your letter came Friday and I was quite pleased to get it. It enlightened me as to what to do.

When I received your card and the nice box of candy at Christmas, I was greatly surprised as well as pleased with it. I wanted to let you know how much I appreciated it, but I did not feel at liberty to write. I feared my letter would not be acceptable and would offend someone else.

Since you stated in your card that you would write later, I decided to wait until I heard from you. I thank you very much indeed for such a nice present, for I am very fond of sweets.

You really gave me an unfair advantage by sending me such a nice greeting under conditions of which I dared not retaliate. However I will try to get even with you in the future, but not under similar conditions — I hope.

I was quite impressed and pleased with the tone of your letter — especially your efforts to improve the opportunities which the Lord will surely give you in this coming year. You may be sure that you will have my most encouraging wishes and help if possible.

We are all liable to be a little careless at times and no matter how good we may be there is always a chance for us to improve. I always have a tender feeling in my heart for the one who says "I will try and do better," and we should avail our efforts to help them.

We have in this city something called the Rescue Mission. It is doing a great deal of good in the way of elevating and saving the poor wretched beings beyond the reach of the churches.

The building they own now was once Smith's Opera House, a place devoted to variety shows where no self-respecting person ever went. It was purchased through the mission through contributions from the people of the city.

The Rescue Mission brings the greatest evangelists in the world here. Because of this, there are a great many families experiencing peace and happiness where there was once drunken wretchedness and poverty. There is one coming soon named Gypsy Jack. He is, as his name implies, a gypsy who was at one time in a band of wandering gypsies. He strayed one time into an evangelistic meeting and was converted. He has since then become an ardent and successful evangelist.

It was indeed very kind of your sister and brother in law to take in and care for the old gentleman through his sickness. If there ever is a time when one appreciates their friends it is when they are away from home and sick. When I was a small boy going to school we used to have a story in one of our readers called "The Valley of Tears," in which was pictured a multitude of people all traveling in one direction. On each one's back was strapped a burden that they were to carry to the end of their journey. The journey represented the journey of life.

One of the features in the story was whenever one person saw another tottering under the burden of life, they would reach out a hand to lighten the load. In the process and at the same time, he would lighten his own. There is great credit due to those who put themselves in trouble and discomfort to help others.

Yes, we had quite a pleasant time at our home this Christmas. I also received a number of nice presents including the one from Battle Creek.

Thank you very much for the permission to call on you. And nothing preventing, I shall avail myself of the opportunity to accept your invitation sometime in the near future. I will let you know beforehand — probably in the spring or summer.

My compositions have been accepted by the E.T. Paul Publishing Company of New York City. I do not know just when they will be published, but when they are, you can be sure that I will send you a copy.

Now Miss Mellinger, I believe I will close for this time. I am thanking you very kindly for your considerate letter and hoping for an early reply.

I remain your friend,

Edwin Ellis

****

Whew! I'm glad they got that worked out, but I still wonder what Estella's beau will think when Edwin shows up. Maybe she already broke up with him, but something tells me we will hear more about him in the future.

A Fire in the Night

Jan. 19, 1909
Battle Creek, Mich.

Kind Friend,

It has been over a week since I received your letter. I intended to answer it sooner but something has hindered me every time. If you will pardon my delay, I will try to do better in the future, for I always like prompt answers to my letters. My partner worked overtime tonight, but I thought of your letter to be answered and I decided not to work.

It is quite warm this evening and rather windy. Strange weather for winter isn't it? I guess they say the skating is good, but I've only used my skates twice this winter. Do you indulge in any outdoor sports?

I attended some musical entertainment at the Congregational Church the other night. It was called "The Messiah," under the direction of Professor Barnes. Have you heard of it? I think it is fine. I heard it once before at the theater and I think it was more complete then. I do love music — especially good band music. I feel sorry for anyone who does not care for music.

I was very glad to get your letter. I missed it very much during our short intermission. I do not think you need to be afraid of offending anyone as long as I answer your letters.

I am glad you enjoyed your candy and you need not feel as though it was unfair or that you are indebted to me for it.

The old gentleman at our house who had typhoid fever is getting along fine. He is about over the fever, but is quite sick yet.

I am glad you plan to call on me in the near future. I hope it will be in spring, because I am not sure I am staying here for the summer. I may go home to Indiana in May or June. My mother wants me to come home to the farm. I suppose she will need me, but I do get so lonesome in the country. I have always lived in town and it seems I can never get used to the country life.

What do you think of local option? I think we will have it here before long. Well, I must close, I am getting sleepy. Looking for an early reply.

I remain Your Friend,

Estelle Mellinger

****

Feb, 8,1909
Battle Creek, Mich.

Friend Edwin,

It has been a few days since I received your letter. Every evening I think I'll answer it when I get home, but then something else takes my attention and I put it off until I get anxious to hear from you again and then I write. I can only imagine it is the same with you, it would be so much nicer if we could see each other and talk face-to-face instead of writing letters, wouldn't it?

By the way Mr. Ellis, you spoke of having fine weather. Well yes, I think it is fine for this time of year, but it can't make up its mind. In the morning we have warm and bright and before nightfall, it will be either raining or snowing to "beat the band."

Today when we went to work we had to wade through about two feet of snow in places. By noon it was raining and this evening it is freezing again with the wind howling around the corners of the house. Tonight it really seems like winter again. I will be glad when spring comes.

I would be pleased to have you come here any time you can and I would also be glad to make a trip over to see your city this summer if the opportunity is granted me. My greatest delight would be to travel. I would love to see Niagara Falls this summer, but I am afraid I can't. Have you ever been there?

I just received a letter today from an old chum in Fort Wayne, Indiana and it makes me a little homesick to see my old friends. She says I should promise to take time off and visit her for a week. If I had my way, I would leave tomorrow, but we can't always have things our way, can we?

We lost a great institution this week. The Haskell Home for Orphans was destroyed by fire last Wednesday night at about 2 o'clock.

And the worst of it was three children were burned and as of yet they have not found their bodies. There were two girls ages 8 and 14 and one boy who was only 9 years of age. They have no clue as to how it caught fire. I used to work there and it makes me very sad.

In your last letter you spoke as though you favored local option. Well I would be more in favor of prohibition because when just some counties or states go dry, the people who drink will send away for their liquor. Then wickedness continues at barbershops and livery stables where innocent young boys are tempted and the parents do not realize these are unsafe places for children.

I think if the whole country went dry it would be a fine thing, but I don't ever expect to see that happen — the world is growing worse instead of better.

Well, I must close or you will get tired of reading. I bid you goodnight.

Ever your friend,

Estelle

****

A few of Edwin's letters seem to be lost, but we can glean from Estella's letters what they are talking about. Never fear, Edwin the writer will soon be back in true form.

A Character Worth Having

Feb. 27, 1909
Battle Creek, Mich.

Kind Friend,

Today is Sabbath and I have just come home from church. Our minister delivered a fine sermon on temperance and spoke especially on local option in our county. He said he hopes all of us will lend our influence in that way. I guess we will have local option over here.

I just read a story in our church paper about a young man who refused to drink with a crowd of men and they asked why he would not drink today as he has always done. He told them a story.

He had stopped by the pawn shop one morning and overheard a conversation between the pawnbroker and a customer which touched him.

The young man had a small package which he handed to the pawn broker saying, "Give me 10 cents." The pawnbroker took it and untied the package and discovered a pair of baby shoes. They had only been worn once.

The broker asked him where he got them and he said his wife bought them for the baby but he wanted ten cents for them so he could buy a drink.

The pawnbroker said he better take them back to his wife. The man said she didn't need them that she had died last night. Then he leaned over the showcase and cried like a child.

The young man whose friends wanted him to drink with them said, "Boys, I have a baby and wife at home and I will not take a drink with you today." If those men only realized the suffering and trouble that drinking causes, they would never take the first drink.

You spoke of loving little children, well I certainly do. You wouldn't believe it if you saw me on my way to church today. I took three little tots to Sabbath school and then I taught a class of little girls from age 8-10. I used to take care of whole families of children from seven to sixteen in a family at the Haskell Home for Orphaned Children a few years ago. They all liked me because I acted like a child with them. I am so saddened by their loss. You must have felt that way when you lost your little sister.

You certainly must be a man with a character worth having. So your musical selections were taken up? I am so glad for I am waiting to get one. I'm more anxious for the vocal selection. I have started to take voice culture. I have always sung alto, but the voice teacher said I have a soprano voice. She was glad I sang alto because it saved my voice. What part do you sing? I certainly like good singing.

The weather is more like winter now, but I am eagerly waiting for spring to show up. This ever changing weather isn't healthy.

I have written enough for this time so I will close.

Looking for an early reply,

Your Friend,

Estelle

March 10, 1909
Grand Rapids, Mich.

Friend Estella,

Your letter came in good time. Now if you will sit down for a few moments I will visit with you, but remember I am to do all of the talking—strange for a man to do, isn't it? I wish it might be verbal instead of by proxy, then I could share the talking with you.

The weather here is very unsettled at present and people are feeling the effects of it. Numerous colds and other such ailments that go with such weather are quite prevalent now. However we have the happy consolation that spring is at hand with more agreeable weather conditions around the corner.

Soon the songbirds will return with their cheerful notes. Next, the wildflowers will show their heads from underneath the green foliage. Then it will seem like the return of an old friend.

If all is well, we may meet then. I should like to see you with your family of little ones at the Sabbath School. You must certainly enjoy it. No doubt you have your hands full at times. It speaks well of you to take so much interest in the church welfare of the little ones.

The forming of higher thoughts in young minds will mean higher virtues by which they will be grounded when they have grown up. I belong to the young men's Bible class of our church and we have a Sabbath school of about 200 members.

You spoke of taking up voice culture, I am glad to hear of it. I think anyone who has a good voice ought to make use of it. My youngest sister is not yet 18 years old, but she has a very clear soprano voice. As the weather gets settled, I intend to have her take vocal lessons. She, like you, is very fond of children and pets of all kinds. She is tender hearted and sympathetic towards every living thing. She thinks a great deal of her big brother and I dare say I do of her — it is one of the things that make my life worth living.

My publishing company wrote me last week to say the first of my compositions, "The Flashlight," will be available in March. The other one will be published later. They are being a little bit foxy because they plan to publish the best one last.

I am holding onto my vocal manuscript until both of my marches are out. I am at present working on a sacred piece which I call, "A Vision," It is something on the order of "The Holy City." I have the words and the melody written, but now I am working on the accompaniment and harmony. This is the hardest part of the work. I hope you may hear it someday. For now, you may look for my first march as soon as it is out.

Now Stella, this is a rather short and uninteresting letter and I am a little ashamed to send it after waiting so long, but I am quite sure you will pardon me this time and you may look for something better next time.

Hoping you will not wait as long as I have,

I remain as always your friend,

Edwin

Shooting to Win

June 22, 1909
Grand Rapids, Mich.

Friend Estella,

I received both of your postcards at once. As you said, I was beginning to wonder if you had forgotten me — or had decided to stop writing. However, I felt if you had decided to discontinue writing you would let me know. I was sorry to hear you have been sick and I hope you are feeling much better by this time. Were you seriously ill?

My mother has been sick but she is much better now.

No, I was not with the troops that passed through Battle Creek. They were on their way to Grand Rapids. What we call the state tryout was held here on our rifle range this year. Last year it was held in Detroit. Everyone in the state militia who has qualified as an expert rifleman is eligible to shoot in this tryout. The fifteen men making the best score are to represent this state at the National in Camp Perry Ohio. Every state in the union does the same thing.

I have qualified for the last three years as an expert, but I am not taking part in the tryout this year. We are very busy in the machine shop. It is all I can do to get away for the encampment which by the way is at Luddington State Park this year. It begins the ninth of August. Next year we are going back to Indianapolis. The War Department figures on sending us every other year to camp with the regulars. I will send you a newspaper clipping which will explain the shoot being held here this week.

Have you heard the "Flashlight" played yet? It needs to be played on the piano because it goes too high for an organ. It is making quite a hit here. A number of the bands and orchestras are playing it and very few know it was written here in Grand Rapids.

The publisher has slated my 6/8 military march for next year sometime. E.T. Paull only publishes two marches each year and one of them is always his own composition.

I have finally finished "The Vision" or I may just call it "Vision" — I am still deciding. It is a semi-classical selection. I have not decided who I will submit it to for publishing yet. I did my best to finish it in time for the Biennial Prize Competition given by the American Federation of Musical Clubs which was held in this city three weeks ago. They gave $1000 for the best orchestra selection and $500 for the best piano solo and the best vocal selection, but I could not get mine completed in time to enter the local competition.

My sister and I attended two of their programs held in the Opera House. We heard the prize orchestra and vocal competition, but I was a little disappointed that I did not get to hear the piano competition.

Well I am not quite satisfied with the deal given me by the publisher. You will noticed they have printed on the cover that it was written by Edwin Ellis and arranged by E.T. Paull — which is not so. As a matter of fact they have made scarcely any change to the piece at all.

Now Stella, in this matter of calling on you, if it is agreeable to you and you feel you would like to get better acquainted with me, I will arrange to call on you someday in the coming month of July — whenever would be most convenient for you.

I think some Saturday would be best since I could make train connections and get back on the same day since we only work a half day on Saturday. We could meet on your Sabbath if it is not objectionable to you and it would perhaps be the most convenient for both of us. If for any reason this is objectionable to you, please say so.

I would also like to ask if by calling on you, I would be intruding on someone else's rights. Or as you asked me one time, would I be butting in on some other young man's privileges? Please let me know about this Stella, for I would not under any conditions, wish to be an intruder.

I have written enough for this time especially since I have not received an answer from my last letter, I trust you will pardon me for taking this liberty.

Hoping to receive an early reply,

I am always,

Your Friend Edwin

****

July 1, 1909
Battle Creek, Mich.

Friend Estella,

I just received your letter today and I will try to be as prompt in answering as you were. I am glad you are feeling better and I hope you will continue to improve until you have fully regained your health. You are fortunate in having your sister near enough so you could be at her home.

I have a great deal to be thankful for in the way of good health. I have not been seriously ill for over fifteen years since I had the black measles. The doctor said I could not have been any worse with the small pox than I was in Chicago that time. I was living with my aunt who took the measles from me and only lived three days. Her husband and three children had them at the same time and it came near being fatal to them too.

Owing to the nature of the disease, none of the neighbors would venture near the house. So I had to care for them alone for three days. I was weak and barely able to get out of bed when they all came down with them at once. I sent a message home to Grand Rapids for my mother who came just a few hours after my aunt died. Meanwhile a Mrs. Calkins who had been a neighbor in another part of the city heard of our troubles and came about the time my aunt died.

Now Estella, as for my plans to come to Battle Creek, I cannot come for the Fourth of July, as I have made arrangements to be at home with my folks. I have promised my mother and sister to go someplace with them and they would be greatly disappointed if I should go away. So if it is agreeable to you, I will make arrangements to come on the twenty-fourth of this month which is on a Saturday.

If it is honorable and also your choice, I may stay over until Sunday. However, we can arrange that later. I will look for the train schedule, so if you wish you may meet me at the depot.

Hoping to hear from you soon,

I am as always your Friend,

Edwin

If Estella was of a mind to put herself first, she might get her nose out of joint because Edwin insists on spending the Fourth of July with his mother and sister. But fortunately, she is not one of Jane Austen's heroines who mistake her lover's good intentions. She seems to understand Edwin's father died when his sister was young and he has been the man of the family for close to ten years. While Edwin deserves his own wife and happiness, he seems to put his mother and sister first. Has he has done the right thing? Will Estella continue to wait patiently? We shall see.

Chicken Hearts and Roller Skates

July 12, 1909
Grand Rapids, Mich.

Friend Estella,

I received your letter — also your postcard which has a very pretty view on it. It resembles a scene in one of our parks here. It gives me the desire to bring my Kodak with me when I come. You know I have been quite a camera fiend. Although I have passed the fiend stage, I still like to take pictures and my camera is often my close companion when I am away from home.

I would much rather go hunting with a camera than a gun. In fact I can see no pleasure or sport whatsoever in going out with a gun to shoot down inoffensive creatures just to see them fall and appease my appetite for wild game. Perhaps I am a little foolish in this way — at least my mother thinks so for I don't have the heart to kill a chicken for her. She has to do all it herself or get one of the neighbors to do it. She says she doesn't see how I can be a soldier if I can't kill a chicken.

I have just sent my vocal manuscript "A Vision" to the publishers. I expect to hear from them soon in regards to publishing it. I read in your letter how you would like to hear me sing it, but you would be disappointed, for I cannot sing. My sister has a very sweet, clear voice, but I am not a good executer of music. I can play just enough to arrange my composition and that is about all. I am just now writing a little march that has been going through my head. Perhaps I can get that finished before I come.

Now Stella, I will look up the train schedule if you still wish to meet me at the depot.

Hoping to get as prompt a reply as I got last time,

I will bid you goodnight,

From Edwin

****

July 17, 1909
Battle Creek, Mich.

Kind Friend,

I guess I will have to be prompt in writing so you can answer before you come.

We have just one week before we finally meet and I am looking forward to it, for I am expecting to have a good time. I am also anxious to meet you for we have been corresponding for over a year and haven't seen each other yet.

I had myself bound to that fellow more by honesty to him, than loyalty to myself. He had habits that were disgusting to me. If I had married him, it might have made my whole life miserable. I have often thought of what you wrote to me after I quit writing to you last winter. The little advice you gave me set me free again.

I am glad you are going to bring your camera along. I had a notion to ask you to bring it. There are some nice views to take here and out by the lake.

Well, since you are no singer, I will excuse you. I will wait until the piece is published and sing it myself.

Well Edwin, you are certainly a chicken-hearted boy. You are as bad as I am, but I wish everyone was like that. The Lord made all these creatures to live and I think anyone who hasn't the nerve to kill them has a natural heart, don't you? But I do agree with your mother. I don't see how you will ever make it as a soldier if you go to war, but I don't think these wars are the right thing anyway.

I went out to the big ball game Thursday between the two lodges, but I did not enjoy the game so much as roller skating. I put skates on for the first time and I did real well—so well that I skated for about two hours and a half. I wouldn't have quit if I hadn't torn my dress, but then I knew it was time for me to quit. I am going again tonight, but I don't know whether I can skate or not, I am so lame I can hardly move today.

This is Sunday morning and I am all in. I was out to the lake skating again last night. I had to get up at 4:30 and iron some clothes. We are packing today and moving. We will be at our new home at 16 Howard St. tomorrow, so I will be looking for a letter telling me when I can meet you.

Bye Bye,

Estelle

I am almost as anxious for Edwin to arrive as Estella is–how strange to talk for a whole year without meeting! When I heard about Edwin's chicken heart, I fell in love with him myself. When I read Estella's remark that "these wars are not the right thing anyway," I realize how much Edwin and Estella's beliefs about kindness to animals and pacifism have formed my own. Their values were passed down through their children and grandchildren to me. I am proud of them for being true to their selves.

Estella Gets an Attitude

Many of Estella's letters are written on stationary with a Kellogg's letterhead. She works in a candy factory which is a part of the famous health institution. It seems a bit ironic, but perhaps this is a foreshadowing of sweet breakfast things to come like Kellogg's Pop Tarts.

After a year of correspondence, Edwin and Estella have finally met, but we don't have any details about the meeting. Since they wrote over a hundred years ago we have no one to fill us in. And even more confusing, we thought Edwin was just coming to see Estella in Battle Creek, but they must have really liked what they saw because it now appears Estella also went to meet his family in Grand Rapids. Love must be in the air because Estella seems to have a new attitude.

****

Kellogg Food Company, Incorporated
"Battle Creek Diet System"

August 13, 1909
Battle Creek, Mich.

Dear Edwin,

I have received two cards from you since I left, but one had a hard time finding me. You put the wrong number on both of them and I guess that is the reason I did not get your first letter.

My old number was 63 Hanover St. but now it is 16 Howard St., so don't forget next time.

Now I wonder if you got my card at camp, as I wrote it Hanah instead of Camp Harrah. I thought it was Harrah but the folks thought it was Hanah. I am going to send this letter to your home and then I know you will get it.

Say please don't sign your name Edd, I don't like it. Call yourself Edwin or I'll have to give you a new name. Ha! Ha!

I guess you think I am a pretty queer girl, giving you orders by the yard. I never did like a nick name – unless it is nicer than the original of course.

I have been working pretty hard these days. I am glad I am through for this week. We quit at noon on Fridays and don't go to work until 8 o'clock on Sunday and then work ten hours a day the rest of the week.

Some friends want me to go fishing with them Saturday night and Sunday but I don't know whether I will go or not. I hate to lose the time.

I suppose it will be quite a while before I see you again. I wish I could see you now and talk instead of writing. I could say so much more, but maybe I have said enough already.

When you come back to Battle Creek, I will give you an answer to the question you asked me.

Our candy kitchen is moving now. I expect we will go to our new work sometime next week.

We will have a new man to make the candy. Mr. Talmage has been asking for a change for a long time. He is now in the shipping department. Well, I must go and iron now so I will say bye, bye.

Yours Truly,

Estelle

16 Howard St.

****

August 17, 1909
Indianapolis, Ind.

Dear Estella,

No doubt you will be surprised to see my letter marked Indianapolis. I am down in your home state. Perhaps this will seem like a letter from home.

Well Stella, I will explain to you how I happened to be in Indiana. I brought my mother here to the Park View Sanitarium to be treated for cancer of the breast. They make a specialty of cancer here — they treat nothing else.

They seem to have wonderful success. My mother's case seems to not be as serious as some. It is a lump on the right breast nearly as large as a cup. Dr. Leach says she can be cured in six weeks to two months.

I do not know just how long I shall be here. I will stay until she feels she can stay the rest of the time alone.

They are a jolly bunch of patients at the sanitarium. No one seems to be downhearted and some of the ones who are in the worst condition are the jolliest ones of all. Each one seems to be making the best of their condition and keeping hope alive.

There is a beautiful park right across the street from the sanitarium. It is called Military Park. The surroundings are so pleasant here people cannot help but enjoy themselves. There is only one thing lacking on my part. I wish you were here.

I suppose the boys in camp are having a good time about now. They start for home on Wednesday. I only went to camp for four days before I came home to bring my mother down here.

Indianapolis is a nice city. I could be quite contented to live here. The lady I boarded with, at one time lived in Lafayette, Indiana, now I am boarding just across the street from the Sanitarium with a Kentucky lady and her son. They are typical Kentuckian—extremely hospitable and friendly, but they have no use for the colored.

So you do not wish me to call myself Edd. Do you like the name Edwin better? Well I guess I will have to abide by my military training to instinctively obey commands. It is said that no man can become a good soldier until he learns to do this. And you know it has always been my ambition to become a good soldier—even though I cannot kill chickens.

I hope you enjoyed your visit to Grand Rapids as much as my folks enjoyed visiting with you. I hope you would like to visit us again sometime. If you feel that you would like me to do so, I will arrange a stopover in Kalamazoo and run over to Battle Creek on my way home from here.

Well Stella, I will not write anymore for this time, but please write soon and often for you know if ever I can appreciate a letter it is now.

From Edwin

Edwin's Day at the Speedway

August 22, 1909
Indianapolis, Ind.

Dear Estella,

You letter came when I had just set out my writing materials ready to write to you because I wanted to talk to someone, and I know of no one I'd rather talk to than you.

There is a beautiful park across the street and when morning comes I wish you were here so I could have someone to sit in the park and visit with. This city, like Grand Rapids, has quite a number of nice parks and other places of pastime and amusement, but I don't think any of them come up to our ball park in Grand Rapids. I might think that I am just partial to my home city if it weren't for the fact that I have heard residents of this city who have been to Grand Rapids say the same thing.

I went out yesterday to the automobile races. They are just completing the new two and one half mile speedway at a cost of $1,000,000. It is considered the finest in the world, but this monstrous project grand as it is, has exacted a heavy toll on human lives.

I reached the Speedway about three o'clock yesterday afternoon. They were just holding the last and most important of the opening events. It was a three hundred mile race between heavy racing machines. Sixteen powerful machines were lined up for a race which many knew would make history in the world of auto racing.

The thundering of the powerful motors all working at once made the ground tremble. Each driver's hand grasped his levers in readiness to send his machine ahead at the signal of the starter. Eventually the signal shot was heard and each driver threw himself on his lever. Some of the machines seemed to leap from the ground in their mad efforts to gain a lead. No efforts are made to muffle the motors in the race and the noise of the thundering machines and the clouds of smoke made a grand comparison to a line of battle in action.

The sixteen powerful speeders were off. The line was quickly broken as some of them forged ahead in the lead. Each machine carried beside its driver a mechanician who is an expert mechanic to make quick repairs in all emergencies.

The puffing, snorting monsters were for a few seconds lost from view as they rounded the farther bend of the large speedway, but only for a moment as they soon came from the opposite direction.

The next strand of the broken line came tearing apart, fairly burning the track beneath it. Each driver, realizing the importance of winning this race, was using every effort known to his skill to add speed to his machine. Lap after lap was played in this manner. Every few minutes saw a previous record smashed to smithereens.

Each machine was numbered, so it was easy to tell them apart. The spectators who had watches held them in their hands timing the different machines. Even the slowest machines were making better than a mile a minute, and some were circling the big track of two and a half miles in two minutes and eight seconds — showing an awful speed of 75-80 miles an hour.

One hour passed and two of the machines dropped out. Then two hours passed, and four more dropped out for repairs, but the other ten kept up the grind.

By this time, the track began to get a little rough from three days of racing, which made the speeding machines bound at times like bucking broncos.

It could be plainly seen the terrible grueling this was taking on the plucky drivers and their faithful mechanicans. Their grim and set faces told only too well the awful physical and nervous strain they were undergoing, yet the grinding pace was kept up.

I was on the inside of the track and at one end, where the track is raised up on a slant to offset the centrifugal force of the machines going around the corner at such a speed. A small creek ran under the track at this point and on the outside of the track was a cement wall two feet high for a distance of eighty feet where the creek ran under.

Suddenly a cry went up from the vast crowd of spectators. In an instant one of the heavy machines was seen to strike the end of the cement wall, bound high in the air and shot out over the heads of the onlookers and landed directly in the crowd burying the mechanician and three spectators. The driver was thrown clear of the machine and escaped serious injury.

They have an emergency hospital on the grounds and their ambulances were immediately called into service and the injured cared for. The machine in its wild flight had injured several more or less, but only three were killed in this wreck.

Wild confusion ruled the crowd for a short time. People ran in all directions looking for friends and relatives, not knowing if they were among the killed or injured. Wives and mothers were frantically searching for husbands and children, but this did not last long.

The sputtering of the speeding motors as they went by soon grabbed the crowd's attention again. Only three had been killed, what of it? They had come to see speed. Just then another cry went up and another machine has gone wrong.

This one struck a post supporting the bridge over the speedway and turned completely over. The mechanician crawled out from under the wrecked machine, but the ambulance which has just reached the hospital with the last victims of the other wreck came hurrying back to get the driver.

The two accidents happened within a hundred feet of each other and right near the grandstand before the eyes of thousands of people.

The remaining eight cars kept up the grind, the drivers realizing that some disaster had happened, yet dare not for an instant take their eyes from their course. Some of them were blinded from the smoke and dirt and had to stop long enough so a physician could wash out their eyes.

One driver was seen to swing his arm around in the air, while he guided his machine with the other in an effort to get life back into his arm which had become numb from the awful vibration of the machine as it sped over the roughened track. On another machine, a mechanician was seen to do the same thing.

"Another one gone wrong!" shouted the crowd, as just around the curve another machine swerved to the left and suddenly leapt clear of the track. Fortunately, it went on the inside of the track and landed right side up in the soft sand which lines the track on the inside.

Up to this time, the daring drivers had been racing with death, but death and injury were gaining such a lead that after a hurried council, the officials signaled the racers to stop and declared the race off.

One after another, the smoking machines were brought to a stop in front of the judges' stand and a pitiful sight it was. Drivers and mechanicians limped and staggered from their machines, some of them crying and holding their hands to their face suffering and half blinded from the dust and smoke in their eyes.

A driver and his mechanician were killed by running into a fence the first day making five killed in all. This driver was a young man 22 years old. His mother begged of him that day not to get into the race, but he assured her that he would come home alright in the evening.

Thus ended three days of what they call spirit. Meanwhile death's grim reaper has had its say and laid bare the lacerated hearts of mothers, wives and other relatives and friends who cared about these people.

Yes, Estella, my sister and her husband are living in our house. The box of candy came and I wrote them to save it for me. I think it will keep alright and I still have a little of the first you sent me and although it is a little harder, it seems to be as good as ever.

With you I am never failing for candy —I thank you very much for it Stella, for I know and appreciate the expense you go to get it for me and the expense of sending it also. Perhaps someday I will do something equally as pleasing to you. I will try.

I am yet undecided as to when I will come home, but I will let you know. If at all possible, I will arrange to come on Friday so I can stop over and see you.

Well I guess I have kept you busy for a while trying to read this letter so if you will excuse the poor writing and mistakes, I will say bye bye for this time.

Write soon and often,

From Edwin

A Day at the Park

August 27, 1909
Battle Creek, Mich.

Dear Edwin,

I am writing about the same time I did a week ago. I make a practice of ironing every Friday afternoon and I have a few minutes to wait while my irons get hot, so this is the way I fill in the time.

It is storming here at present, but I hope it will clear off before tomorrow morning. I want to go to Camp Meeting, I already bought my ticket, but it if rains, I won't want to go.

Camp Meeting is being held in Jackson and I am glad for the chance to spend one day there. Our church has two or three Camp Meetings in each state. I wish you were here to go along with me.

Too bad you are so far away. I would rather visit face-to-face with you any day than have to write. I would love to be with you in Indianapolis, Edwin, but we both know that is impossible.

Never mind the expense of that candy, I got it free and I am glad you are enjoying it. You have repaid me a dozen times in friendship and I am always glad to do anything for anyone who appreciates it.

You are a jewel! Ha! Ha!

How is your mother getting along? I hope she is improving rapidly. We can never do too much for our parents.

Well, I guess I will go and iron now and finish writing this evening.

Here I am again, but it is late, so I won't write much. I am awful tired and sleepy and have to get up early in the morning so if you will pardon me, I will make it short but sweet.

I got your card the other day. That Speedway is a great thing, but I think it is terrible to put so much money into an amusement that actually kills people. There are enough murders and suicides, but this is the worst of all.

I have started to copy your piece of music (that Indiana song) for my brother at home and he is getting anxious to see it, but I don't have much time to copy it. I took it over to a friend's house the other evening and my cousin played it and I sang it. Then Mr. Talmage our foreman played with her on the mandolin. It sounded just lovely.

I wish I were home now, then I could come over to Indianapolis real easy. You are only about 50 miles from my home. Well dear, I will say goodnight and try to write more next time.

Estella

August 31, 1909
Indianapolis, Ind.

Dear Estella,

I received your letter last evening and even though it was short and sweet, you may be sure I was pleased to get it. If ever I have appreciated letters from home, it is now and it always seems like a letter from home when you write.

Yes, I feel as you do. It would be much nicer if we were nearer to each other so we could visit instead of writing. Who knows what the future has in store for us? Perhaps we may someday. It's up to you, Stella.

Did you have a nice time at camp meeting? Or did it storm, so you could not go? I should have liked so much to have been there with you.

I am working in an automobile factory down here. It is called the Nordyke and Marmon Company. They pay me 3.50 per day, but oh such work. I have a much better and fine class of work at home. When I get into an automobile shop it is like going back into a machine shop again.

The first job they gave me to do was a jig for drilling out a part of the steering gear which someone else had tried to make and spoiled, so I had to make it over and patch it up as best I could. I would much rather make it up from the beginning than patch up someone else's botch job. However, they seem to be nice people to work for.

Stella, I wish you were here to see what an interest this city takes in the physical hygiene training of its children.

All the parks have different kinds of gymnasium appliances for the little folks to perform on and each park has a matron to look after the little ones and two training teachers — a man to teach the young boys and a lady instructor to teach the little girls.

They have running and jumping and performing on the parallel bars. And a game for the girls called captain ball and another which they call tether ball. Both of these games require great activity especially the latter.

Tether ball is played by two girls at one time. A pole is set about ten feet high. At the top of the pole is fastened a string while on the other end of the string is a ball which hangs about two feet from the ground. The contestants are armed with a tennis bat with which to strike the ball. Each one tries hitting the ball to wind the string around the pole in the opposite direction of her opponent and vice versa. When one hits the ball and it starts to wind around the pole, the other tries to strike it and wind it back the other way.

Some of the little girls become quite proficient in this game and it is certainly interesting to watch them. Once a year they have a day they call children's field day (usually held at Garfield Park) where all the schools come together with their respective trainers. They have contests in all the exercises they practice throughout the summer.

This year the event was held yesterday at Garfield Park and I was invited by some of the instructors to take photographs of the different events. Over one thousand children took part in it. The colored children were well represented also. Kite flying is also an event and the one whose kite flew the highest won a prize.

During the warm weather, they have a bathing place set up. They have different days set apart — one schedule for the little boys, and days set aside for the little girls. The lady class instructors are all good swimmers. It is one of the accomplishments necessary to become an instructor whether they are a man or woman. I was invited to watch both of their classes and I was surprised to see the number of girls that can swim and dive equal to the little boys.

Well Stella, I will have to close since I am working now and will have to get up early. The band is playing across the street in the park. If you were only here, I would not be writing, now would I?

Write quickly,

Goodnight Stella,

From Edwin

Desperate for Mail

September 8, 1909
Indianapolis, Ind.

Dear Estella,

You can scarcely imagine how pleased I was when I came home from work and found your letter awaiting me. While the people here are kind and friendly, I get awful homesick to see someone from home. And as you say, it seems like a long time between letters.

Yes, it would be nice if you were at your Indiana home now, but it would be equally as nice if you were here. I dare say however, that there is a father and mother down this way who would like to see their girl and who perhaps wonder when they will see her again. To them I would surrender all rights and privileges to see her first, but I should like very much to have the next quiet little visit with her. I wonder if she would enjoy it as well as I would?

There is one thing down here in Indianapolis that would especially please you, and that is the children's aid association that I wrote about. The instructors are so kind and pleasant to their little charges that one believes they must love their work and the little ones seem to think much of their instructors.

Before I went to work, I spent a great deal of time at the children's aid association and made lots of friends among the little folks. I went out Saturday afternoon and took a picture of the whole bunch of them.

After I had taken the picture, they all had a curiosity to look through my camera. So I focused it on the children's merry go round, and had them all stand in line and let each one get under the focusing cloth to look at the image of the merry go round in motion on the ground glass. There were about two hundred of them so you can know I had quite a job on my hands. One little boy wanted me to turn the camera over since they were all standing on their heads.

The matrons and instructors said I must have lots of patience to take the time and trouble to do it, but it was well worth the time and trouble to see the delight it gave the little ones and to hear the funny remarks that some of them would make.

I meant to tell you Stella, when I wrote before that you need not hurry to copy my song. I have written out another copy of it so you may keep it until I come, or until I send for it. I am glad your friends like it. I expect to be here at least six weeks longer. The doctors think they can have Ma cured by that time. I hope it will not be any longer.

Belva, my youngest sister, is still out on the farm yet and they do not seem to want to let her go, so I don't know whether we will be able to claim her anymore or not when we return. Did she write to you yet? She sent to me for your address so I suppose she has written by this time or will soon.

No Stella, this is not a very interesting letter, I admit it, but it will be acceptable just the same, will it not? And I will make a better effort next time.

So I will bid you good night from

Edwin
P.S. I know you will write soon without asking, won't you?

September 13, 1909
Battle Creek, Mich.

Dear Edwin,

After eagerly watching for a letter every day, you know how glad I was when it came. I am sitting in the parlor with my big, black cat on my lap writing to you. It is so awful sultry and warm tonight I can't find a comfortable place to sit. I wish you were here to sit in the park with me.

I certainly would enjoy a quiet visit with you dear, but it seems that it cannot be now. And the worst of it is I don't know when it will be.

I am left alone now with all the girls in the candy kitchen, and of course they all look to me and depend on me for everything. I am kept pretty busy both mind and body.

I am really getting homesick to see my dear ones at home, but I will have to stand it until after Christmas and then I will make a great effort to go home.

The schools opened today and my brother is sending his oldest boy to church school. He thinks he is going to church every day. You can't hardly make him understand, he is only six years old.

Oh yes, Edwin, you are a children's friend alright, and everybody else's too, but you are my best friend, aren't you?

Yes Edwin, I received a nice card from both of your sisters. I presume they are getting pretty lonesome to see you and your mother again. You are having quite a stay there.

Well, the girls at the factory want me to copy a song for them — The Black Sheep. So I think I will be ready for bed by that time.

Now please write soon, for I am as anxious as you are to get a letter.

So good night,

Estelle

You Might Get Tired of Me

September 15, 1909
Indianapolis, Ind.

My Dear Stella,

I came home from work at 6:30 o'clock and found your letter waiting for me. It is now 8 o'clock and I am sitting in my room writing an answer to it.

Making fairly good time for me, isn't it? But perhaps I have slightly selfish motives in view. You see, the sooner you get my answer, the sooner I get a letter from you. You don't blame me for that, do you Stella? But it is just as much of a pleasure for me to write to you as it is for you to get my letters. For this is the nearest we can get to visiting with each other when we are so far apart. And it is equally as great a pleasure to me to know that my letters are always welcomed until such time as you should see fit to have them stopped, but I don't believe you will do that, will you?

Yes Stella, I have made many friends among the little ones here, and also many friends among the grown up people for as I have said before, I find the Hoosier's a very friendly class of people. But if it is your wish, I will place you at the head of the list and be as you say the best friend to you!

I am still working in the tool room at the automobile factory, but I do not like the work very well. I have been used to a great deal finer and cleaner and better class of work than making tools for auto building.

At the Grand Rapids Brass Company, we all have stools and can sit down at our work whenever we wish. Here we have no stools and we are not allowed to sit down from morning to noon and from noon until night. I am not used to this and it makes my feet ache and pain me so that it seems I can scarcely wait for six o'clock. Sometimes they ache after I go to bed until I can scarcely sleep.

The first job they gave me was a job for drilling some holes in the steering gear. Another man had worked on it for two weeks and had it so badly mixed up that he could not see his way out, so he quit to save himself from getting fired.

The foreman gave me the job to finish, saying there was not much more to do on it. When I began to size it up and call his attention to a few things that did not look right to me, he said several words that would not look well in writing.

Then he wound up saying, "I wonder who ever told that fellow he was a tool maker?" I had to do the whole job over again using such parts he did not spoil.

I will certainly be glad when I can get back up to Grand Rapids to my old job. I got a letter from the foreman saying my wages have been raised.

I'm afraid, Stella, that you are working yourself too hard both physically and mentally at your work. You know the Lord has made our physical bodies to stand quite a bit, but he has also placed a limit on how much we can endure. If we over step this limit, nature is liable to retaliate and we have to suffer for it. One is quite apt to over step this limit when they are overloaded with responsibilities.

There is a man working in this shop on the bench next to me who is a periodical drinker — that is, he gets drunk once about every four weeks. It lasts him about four days and when he comes back to work he is a pitiful sight to see. His eyes are sunken in, his cheeks are hollowed and his hands tremble. In fact, he is a nervous wreck for a week after. He has a wife and six children.

I wonder what must be the feeling of the poor wife when she sees him in that condition and knows that her little ones are living witnesses to the sad spectacle of their father in his drunken wretchedness. My heart aches for this unfortunate woman and many others in the same condition.

I'm afraid in this case and a great many others, it is a case of marrying in hopes of reforming afterward. If it was only the man and wife that had to suffer for this mistake, it would be bad enough, but when they bring children into this world to suffer for their actions, they are adding to the wound a great many times.

Well Stella, I don't know if this letter is any improvement over the other ones, but you'll appreciate it all the same, won't you?

Trusting that you will write right away,

I wish you good night,

From

Edwin

September 27, 1909
Battle Creek, Mich.

Dear Edwin,

I received your letter Sabbath and this is Monday night so I guess I will have to write you — that is, if I want to hear from you again.

I don't feel very well tonight. I have taken an awful cold. It has been so cold in the candy kitchen and they are so busy they haven't found time to put in the steam coils yet.

My head roars like the sea, so if I make any mistakes or if you find my letter short or uninteresting, please excuse it.

Joe and Edith have gone to the theater tonight and left me to take care of the children. I just put the baby to sleep and all is quiet and lonesome now. I wish you were here with me to keep me company. I feel rather nervous all alone.

I was quite surprised to hear that your mother had an operation, although I cannot see how they could do her any good without it. I can sympathize with her, yet an operation seems pretty good when it saves one's life. Give her my love and tell her I think of her often and hope she will get along alright.

I just read in the paper that Indiana felt earthquake shocks this morning. Did you notice it? It makes me shudder when I hear of so many earthquakes. It shows plainly that this old earth will not stand much longer.

I am actually getting homesick to see my folks. I think I will try to get off for a few days and go home. Say, if I should take the notion to go while you are in Indiana, will you come over to Lafayette to my home to see me? If you will promise to do that, I will try to go in a couple weeks, because I won't be able to go until after Christmas rush is over at the candy kitchen and that seems like a long time to wait. I don't suppose you will stop here on your way home because you will need to go on with your mother, or do you intend to stop anyway?

I sent your sisters each another card the other day, I haven't written them any letters yet.

Well I guess you aren't very jealous of the children, are you? Most children do like me for some reason or another. I don't know why. I don't make much over the children, yet when they come my way, I try to make it pleasant. I generally treat people as they treat me. You say I act rather reserved and some are half afraid of me. Well, I do act so with some people and some I don't. It is just as they act toward me. If you would see me sometimes, you would change your mind a little.

I wish I could be with you more so we could get better acquainted with each other's ways. You can't learn a person's likes and dislikes and their ways all in a minute. You might get tired of me if you were with me after a while and then you might not; we can't always tell. They say distance makes the heart grow fonder, but I don't know if it is true in our case. I think we ought to get better acquainted, don't you?

Well, I think I've said enough for a girl like me, so I will close.

Ever Yours,

Estelle

One wonders how long these lovers will stay apart. Estella seems afraid to commit to marriage until she feels they know each other better. Edwin seems to hint of marriage a couple of times saying it's up to Estella if they will see each other more often. Lovers today can simply text each other and get an answer within a few seconds, but alas poor Edwin and Estella must continue to wait by the mailbox hoping for a letter. And even when a letter comes, they really don't know each other that well so it will be a miracle if they finally get together and stay together.

Two Mysterious Candies

October 6, 1909
Indianapolis, Ind.

Dear Estella

Your letter came to me this morning, and as today is Wednesday I will try to write back so you can get it by your Sabbath. I think of you every Saturday and wish I were there to keep you company.

I am sorry that you cannot get away to visit your folks. I know your father and mother must have a longing to see their children when they have been away from home for so long. I should like to have met your folks.

No doubt you feel more tied down now that you have more responsibility at work. It really seems that they are asking too much of you to look after so many and do your own work. I am afraid you will not be able to keep up under it all.

I am glad you are feeling better again. You must take care of yourself, for I want to see you well when I call on you.

Ma and I are making calculations on starting for home on Friday, the 15th of the month.

We will start from here in the morning. I will stop off at Kalamazoo and some of my folks will meet my mother in Grand Rapids, so I will be at your place sometime Friday afternoon if nothing happens to prevent it.

I think your foreman must have been guessing at what he said about your getting married.

I will certainly be glad to get back to good old Michigan again. Although I must say that Indiana has all one could want in a state. Everyone is so friendly and hospitable than one cannot help but feel at home here.

I think I told you that the lady I am boarding with is Kentuckian and she is typical of the people from her state — extremely friendly, and kind-hearted to all who appreciate it, but resentful to anyone who might do her or anyone else an injury.

However, she has been very kind to my mother and has taken a great deal of interest in making it pleasant for her since she has been here. After my mother's operation, Mrs. Phelps went in to visit her every day and took her such nice flowers.

Well, Estelle, I will not try to write too much this time, but I will wait until I see you then make up for what I don't write.

Write as soon as you get this so I will have time to make a reply in case I should make any different plans on my way home.

Good Night,

Edwin

Oct. 22, 1909
Grand Rapids, Mich.

My Dear Estella,

Your letter came today, and like you, I had to read it before I ate, so I took it to the supper table with me and read while the rest were eating. My folks jollied me and my brother-in-law said that if he was in my place, he would do the same thing.

I certainly would like to have been somewhere near when you went to your work after leaving me the day I came home. I regret that I should be the cause of any embarrassment to you in that way. However, Estella if they all showed a friendly freedom toward you enough to jolly you, it shows that you are well thought of and well-liked by your shop mates. What did the little girl that watching for us at the interurban station have to say?

I opened the box of candy you gave me on the way home. When I got on the train at Kalamazoo for Grand Rapids, I ate some of it on the train.

After I got home, I found the two mysterious little candies. I ate one of them and now I am saving the other for future use. I am guessing no longer.

Well Estella, this is now Monday, and I am still finishing this letter. I am on the company board of directors at the armory. We had a board meeting last night and it was long. By the time I got home, it was so late that I did not have time to finish your letter.

I have finished up each of the pictures I took down there. The one of your sister's folks on the front porch is as I was afraid, out of focus. I did not have my camera set tight enough and it slipped back. As for the others, you can find how many of each your brother's and sister's folks want and how many of each you want. Just let me know when you write.

So, you do not like to write anymore? Well, it does seem like a rather remote way of visiting after being together. However, I would feel awfully lonesome if I could not hear from you every few days.

Now Estella, in regards to coming to see you, if you are not superstitious, I will come on Friday November 12th, then visit with you on Saturday the 13th. Or if you would rather, I will wait until the 20th. It is all the same with me.

I called at the shop the second day I got home, and Mr. Sinclair, the head of the company called me into his office. He asked me when I was coming to work. I said when my tool box arrived since it seemed to be delayed. So he extended the long distance phone and called up the Marmon Auto Co. in Indianapolis and found out that through a mistake my box had not been shipped yet.

It came the next day at noon. I asked him how much for the long distance phone call and he said four hundred dollars.

I told him that was more money than I had. He laughed and said if I could not pay that, I need not pay anything. You ought to see the work they had piled up on my bench waiting for me. The foreman told one of the men that if I did not come back soon, they would be in trouble because I was the only one who had the figures on them. The boys in the shop were as pleased when I came back as they were at the armory.

Everything seems nice and pleasant now that I am home. There is only one thing lacking and you know what that is.

Belle just came home today. She has been visiting her cousin who is about her age and married. They came home with her today and insisted that Belle go back with them, but Ma said she wanted her kids with her some of the time. Belle asked me why I did not bring Stella home with me. I told her it takes two to make a bargain and I am only one.

Now Estella dear, this letter is not much better than the other for all I promised it to be. I can think of lots of things to say, but I want to talk to you — so they will wait until I see you again.

Write soon and often,

Good night with love from

Edwin

****

I wish I knew what those two mysterious candies looked like. Did they say "I do?" Were they some symbol of love, like a heart or two love birds? I wonder if anyone else in the family has heard of these candies, but my guess is that Edwin and Estella are the only ones who know and they took their secret with them.

I guess we can forgive them for not describing these candies, because without their letters, Edwin and Estella would just be two more mysterious names in the family tree.

An Unsealed Letter

Oct. 26, 1909
Battle Creek, Mich.

Dear Edwin,

I knew I would hear from you today. I told the girls I would get some letters and I got two besides the pictures.

I had to read your letter first, but by the time I read yours, and one from my brother, and then looked at the pictures, I did not have much time to eat.

I took the pictures to the factory and they all thought they were fine. They all wanted the one with Esther and I on the log. So I guess I will have a dozen of them. My brother wants a half dozen of the boys and baby on the porch.

I just sent them out to my sister to see what she wants, but first of all, how much are they? How much do they cost? I will tell you later how many my sister wants.

I am tired and sleepy, so I hope you can read my writing tonight. I guess you can't help but see that I am rattled by the thought of writing this letter. I was out late for four nights in succession and I have to go to bed early tonight.

You really should have been here last night. All the candy girls and their husbands all went out to May Dingma's home for a good time and we went on a wild goose chase after my dress. Some dressed in little girls short dresses.

One dressed like a ghost and I dressed as "Johnny on the spot" — ha ha! I dressed as a boy and had my hair all covered with a short hair wig. No one would know but that I was a boy.

It was fun for the whole crowd. May says she wishes you were here to take my picture. Maybe you wouldn't like to see me cutting up such capers — you do not know what a silly kid I am.

We all had a lovely time with music and singing and games. We also had apples and popcorn and cake for refreshments.

Well, Edwin, I would have liked to have gone home with you when you left, but I cannot always do as I please. I want to get my sanitarium bill paid first. It will take me until New Year's Day to be free.

I feel rather tired of the busy factory tonight. We have two or three days of the week to make four or five different kinds of candy. It is always a hard day for me to divide all the work and keep all the girls busy.

Edwin, your date is alright with me. I am not superstitious about anything. Just the 12th is a long way off, but we must write often to cheer each other up.

I guess I have written enough as it is so I will bid you goodnight with love,

Estelle

P.S. Say Edwin, your letter had never been sealed — no signs of it on the envelope, and it was wide open.

Oct. 28, 1909
Grand Rapids, Mich.

Dear Estella,

Your letter came today and as usual I had to read it before I ate my supper. I felt sure I would find one when I came home from work. I also received a pretty postcard last Monday. There was no writing on it except the address but there was a dainty little picture on it which told a story plainer than the reader could have written in words. In fact I could almost imagine a young lady watching and waiting for someone.

I went out to the rifle range last Saturday afternoon and finished up my qualifications as an expert rifleman. I had finished all rangers up to the 800 and 1000 yard and the skirmish fire before I went away.

The captain went out with me. I was as tickled as a little boy with a tin whistle for every expert counts 200% in the company's figure of merit. Sharp shooter counts 100 and marksman 50. When I ran my skirmish it was so dark that you could see the fire spit from the muzzle of my rifle. I got 12 hits out of 20 for the figures on the target. The captain said that was never equaled on the range before at that time of day.

The state has just issued us new olive drab uniforms. I expect we will be all swelled up with pride when we get them on.

I am glad your folks liked the photographs so far, and I will try and make them up this week—at least what you have ordered. I was a little disappointed in some of them. They did not come out as good as I wished them to. I will tell you the price of them when I have them all finished and sent to you.

I should like to have been there and seen you all dressed up in boys clothes so I could laugh at you. If nothing happens to prevent it, I will be there to see you on Friday the 12th. Then I can tell you lots of things that I cannot write.

Ma says to thank you very much for the beautiful postcard you sent. She thinks it is very pretty.

Well, Estella, I will write as you say little and I will send this in the morning so you can get it by your Sabbath for you will be looking for it then. I surely must have forgotten to seal your last letter, but I thought for sure I did. I will try and not be too careless in the future.

Write soon and often. Be sure to give my best to your brother and sister and families. Tell them I appreciate very much their kind and friendly hospitality to me while I was there.

Yours with love,

Edwin

Carved by a Knife

Nov. 3, 1909
Grand Rapids, Mich.

Dear Estella,

Your letter came yesterday and I tried to answer it but one of my cousins and her husband came and stayed the evening with us. By the time they left, I was too tired to write any kind of letter to my little girl that would be presentable.

Night before last was drill night at the armory. After the drill, we had a party and supper and I did not get to bed until 12 o'clock and that left me very tired last night.

Now Estella, I should like very much to be with you on the 11th to attend the surprise party for your brother's wife. I have no doubt I would enjoy myself and you would no doubt find me as big a kid as any of you. But I am afraid it is as much as I can do to get away on Friday the 12th. I will be thinking about you at that time, however, and hoping you are having a good time.

No, Stella, there never would be any war in our home between you and me with your big knife and my rifle. For if I should happen to see the big knife coming for me, I would throw my rifle and run, then you would have them both and the fight would be very unequal.

With our rifles, it would do me no good to get behind a tree for they will shoot through forty inches of wood and I would stand no chance in the open against your big knife.

Then too, think of the nice little morsels of candy you might be making while you are carving me up in little pieces and getting them ready to dip. No candy knife for me. Then supposing sometime in the future in your sleep, you should get to dreaming that you are cutting candy —oh yes, I could see my finish!

It might stand me wise to return all the knives and scissors before returning—otherwise I might awake in the morning minus all my toes and fingers and find them all nicely dipped in chocolate and laid up to dry.

By the way, I have just eaten the other mysterious little candy that you put in the box for me.

If I make many mistakes and have poor writing you will have to excuse me for I have a cold like your sister had while we were out there and I can readily sympathize with her. I will finish your pictures up some time this week.

Say Stella, I have launched on another piece of music. I have tackled something this time that I have never tried before. It is a waltz. Do you like waltz music? It is for my best little girl if I can ever finish it. Do you know who she is? Ha! Ha!

Well my dear, this letter is short, but I will write you often to make up for it. Write soon and often.

Good night with love and affection,

From Edwin

Nov. 6, 1909
Battle Creek, Mich.

Dear Friend,

I received your letter yesterday and since I have a few minutes before church time, I will write a line or so. I wish you were here to go to church with me.

I am in a poor mood for writing just now, so if you find this an uninteresting letter, consider the source. It is raining part of the time and then the sun shines and I feel like the weather.

So you think I will have to do all the fighting when we have war, do you? Well I feel sorry for you if you can't play your own part, poor little boy. Ha! Ha! No danger of fighting in my sleep, it is when I am awake that I do all my carving. But I never hurt anyone yet.

Four or five of us girls went to the Salvation Army Meeting and it was given out that there would be several great speakers from out of town, and of course we expected to hear something great. Well, of all shows and clowns, they were there. I thought I would have hysterics before I got out of there.

Now Dearie, this will be the last letter I write before you come, but I expect a letter from you this week. I guess my brother won't have that surprise for Edith. The baby is sick and so is Frank, so Edith is going to take them to the doctor this afternoon.

You must get rid of your cold so that you feel good.

Lovingly, Estelle

Stealing Kellogg's Candy Recipe

Nov. 9, 1909
Grand Rapids, Mich.

Estella Dear,

Your letter came yesterday. Last night was drill night and it was so late when I got home that I didn't even attempt to answer it, so this will be just one day late in coming.

Well, Stella, it will only be three more days before I see you so I will not write very much, but wait until I get there – then I will make up for what I do not write. Then perhaps you will wish I had written more and not talked so much.

My cold is getting better; I think I will be alright by Friday. I am sorry that your brother was not able to give the surprise to his wife and also that the little ones are sick. I do hope their illness will not be of a serious nature.

We are all quite well here and Ma is getting along nicely. I will bring your pictures with me when I come.

Now, Estella dear, please excuse this letter and just wait until we see each other. My folks all send their love to you. Walter said to send his too, and I told him not much – that I don't want to hear of his sending any love to you.

Good Night,

With love, From Edwin

Nov. 15, 1909
Grand Rapids, Mich.

My Dear Estella,

I just got home from drilling at the armory. It is half past eleven o'clock but if I wait until tomorrow night, you may become anxious and wondering what is wrong with Edwin.

Well, my dear, I reached Kalamazoo in quick time yesterday and waited nearly an hour for the Grand Rapids train. I met one of the corporals from our company at Kazoo. He and his wife, and two little ones were just coming from Battle Creek by train and were waiting for the same train I was.

I found the box of candy excellent company coming home. You have no idea how much I appreciated it this time. I managed to save a very few pieces for Belle. She said if I had a few more miles, she would not get any. I think Stella, you should get the formula for making it, then you can make it for your own use in the future.

What did they say to you this time in the candy kitchen when you went to work? I am anxious to know.

Tell Mae that I did not mean to be discourteous to her on Sabbath at the church, but we left in such a hurry that I did not have time to talk to her.

Belle went with Aunt Tote up to Grant today. She says when I write again to give her love to her future sister. If you accept all the love that is sent you, where are you going to find room for mine? You will have to keep a cozy little corner reserved, I guess.

Now, Stella dear, this is not much of a letter and poorly written, so just make the best of it that you can and write right back.

With love and affection,

Edwin

Jealous of the Armory

November 17,1909
Battle Creek, Mich.

Dear Edwin,

I was so glad to get your letter today. I thought you waited long enough and then it was short enough too. I tell you, I am getting jealous of that armory business. I wish you would lose your interest in it pretty soon. I suppose I am a little selfish, but it doesn't interest me as much as some other things.

If you like fighting so well, you will learn enough about fighting when I come up there. We can go through the drill as often as you like and maybe sometimes oftener. I'll make a good soldier once I get started.

I am glad you enjoyed your candy, but you are a bit stingy with it, aren't you? Never mind, tell Belle I will bring her a box all for herself when I come.

Yes, I think I can make the candy myself alright, but I have never tried yet. We can send for some every once in a while, can't we?

Well, my dear, you wondered how I would be welcomed at the candy kitchen, my foreman saw me coming from a distance and stood in the door of the factory waiting for me. When I got up to him, I asked him what the matter was. He said he was wondering if they would get their girl back again. I said yes, you can't lose a bad penny so easily.

All afternoon, the boys one by one would bring me in a postcard, then yesterday all day too and today I got two more. I told them I will have to have a new album just for them; I got about twelve in all. They tease me all day long. I should think they would get tired of it before long.

I went over to see the doctor today, and I am going to take a month's treatment, and then I will feel good again. I feel better than I did already.

Well you can love my new sister for me until I come and I will have a cozy corner for you. I have lots of room for love, so don't worry sweetheart — I won't forget you.

Oh dear, Joe is here bothering me. I never can write to you in peace but never mind, I won't have to write for long. Yet it seems like a long time to wait to see you. Well, I am going to close now and say goodnight.

Love to all and the biggest share for you,

Estelle

****

November 19, 1909
Grand Rapids, Mich.

My Dear Estella,

I got your letter this evening, and as usual, I had to read it at the supper table. I also got my usual roasting. My folks said your letter was my dessert and that I took my dessert first.

No, Stella dear, you need not be jealous of the armory. It is a long ways from coming ahead of you. It is the only outside pleasure I indulge in and the only night of the week that I am out. Now I am quite a good boy, am I not?

Ma says she is glad you don't like the armory. She will have some help when you get here to scold me for going to it. I think I see my finish at the armory.

I am glad you have decided to take the treatments, for I think they will be beneficial to you. I am also glad you are feeling better than you were when I was there.

We are making all plans and calculations on your being with us on New Year's Day. This is the day that Ma always plans to have her family at home with her.

Bird says she is glad to have a chance on someone to get back for the way we teased her when she got married. And Walter says I certainly have his sympathy, for he has been through the mill and knows all about it.

Once when he came to see Bird, Belle accidentally sat down on his derby hat and smashed it flat. Next time he came he brought a soft cap so Belle could sit on it all she wanted and not damage it. He argued that Derby hats were a little too expensive for cushions, besides there are other things just as comfortable to sit on.

I am going out to the country to my uncle's tomorrow to see about that cutting box, then I will write to Mr. Foote. I have not had a chance to see my uncle since I was there.

Belle is still out to Grant with her Aunt Tote. Ma just got a letter from her today. She is having a jolly time helping Uncle Will on the farm. Whenever they go anywhere with the horses, she goes too. She is like you. She likes horses and likes to drive them. So if I should ever fall heir to a horse, I should have no trouble in finding a driver, would I?

I should like to see the postcards you got at the factory. I bet they are a select lot. Did the couple we met on the street have any select comments about us?

Well Stella, if your friends did not think anything of you, they would not roast you. No doubt about it, it is nothing we have not done to others, so we should expect to take our share when our turn comes.

Your brother Joe certainly must be quite a tease to you, but he is also a good brother to you, so I think well of him for that.

Well Stella dear, I do not seem to be able to write any more long interesting letters to you — my visits with you seems to spoil that. I keep thinking all the time that I wish I was talking instead of writing. I keep counting the days ahead and think I can write much more. However, as you say, we will write often to make up for it.

Give my best wishes to your folks there and love to yourself and write quick!

With love from
Edwin

A Lonely Thanksgiving

Nov 23, 1909
Battle Creek, Mich.

Dear Edwin,

If the folks will go to bed and leave me alone for a few minutes, maybe I can write to you. Edith says I should ask you if you have as hard a time writing a letter as I do. Here it is almost 9:20 and I have had the paper and pencil out for nearly an hour and just got started.

Well you were saying you were glad I was feeling better and I am right now but I have been awful sick since I wrote. I started down town last Friday afternoon and got as far as the park and went in a store and fainted and had to go home in a hack.

I was sick all forenoon but I worked anyway and when I got home, Joe found a doctor at the San and he sent a nurse over to give me some treatments. I was in bed until Monday. Monday evening, I went downtown and to the San for treatment. I tell you, I will miss the San when I leave here, but I hope I won't have much use for it after I leave.

I went back to work today and everybody was glad to see me, but they all said I better not come back. The foreman said I was sick, yet did not want to own up to it. He said I better rest up this week, but of course, they don't know that every day counts with me until Christmas. I am feeling pretty good tonight. I worked all day today, and plan to work tomorrow, then we all lay off until Sunday, so I am glad I went back today.

How is Belle's health nowadays? I am anxious to see her. Tell her I said she could be a sister to me, alright.

I have written for my mother to come up and stay a month with me in December, but I don't know whether she will or not. I am so anxious to see her.

Yes, my dear, we will have to take the teasing too. We were just as ready to tease others so we must take our own medicine. I will send you one of the postcards I got. It is one of the nicest I got, and it is just the kind to send you.

Well, I have written enough for now. Wish I was with you Thanksgiving Day. I suppose you will have a nice time. I expect to, so I will bid you a sweet goodnight.

Lovingly, Estelle

P.S. Don't eat too much turkey!

****

Nov. 25, 1909
Grand Rapids, Mich.

My Dear Estella,

I was a little disappointed when I came home last evening and did not find a letter waiting for me. However, today is Thanksgiving, so I watched for the mailman. When I saw him coming up to our mailbox, I felt much better, for I felt sure of what he was leaving. And the postcard? I believe I like it the best of any you have sent. Whoever sent it to you must have known your sentiments quite well.

No, Estella, no one ever bothers me when I am writing to you, for I always come up here in my den where I have my writing desk and my writing material all by my lonesome. However, I get my teasing when I come downstairs. Bird says it does her good to get back on me for what I did to her. And Auntie Pelton, the neighbor lady you met here, was just in to do her share of roasting to me.

My den has a dormer window facing the East where you can see over a good share of Grand Rapids. I am glad I will soon have someone to share my den and view with me. Then this lonely writing will be a thing of the past, won't it?

Now, Stella dear, I regret very much to hear of your illness. I felt quite encouraged when you wrote before that you were feeling better. And now, Stella, listen to me. Do not work if you are not able or you do not feel like it. As you say, every day may count with you now, but your health counts more! I would rather assume all your financial affairs than to have you work yourself sick. It may take longer to settle things financially, but time will do it, so be careful my dear, and use good judgment.

I hope your Mamma will come to see you — that will do my little girl as much good as any treatment.

Belle is getting along just fine. She goes somewhere for a ride most every day. Ma got a letter from her today and she says she is enjoying herself greatly. I will tell her what you said.

I wish you had been here today — then I would have had even more to be thankful for, but don't forget New Year's. You won't forget, will you, Stella? Belle will be home then and there will be two crazy kids finally together now, won't there be girlie?

I have your waltz nearly finished. It nearly racks my brain to think up strains that harmonize with the sentiments I wish to express in the music. A waltz is a new venture for me as this is my first attempt.

Now, my dear, write as soon as you can, for I shall be anxious to know how you are. Be good to my little girl, for I want to see her at her best when she comes up here for New Year's Day.

Give my best wishes to all of your folks and love to yourself,

With love and affection,

Edwin

P.S. In two weeks, I will be able to help you more with some of your expenses.

Character Readings That Clash

Dec. 4, 1909
Battle Creek, Mich.

My own dear Edwin,

I wrote you a letter last night as soon as I got yours, but it did not look neat enough to send to my sweetheart. I had been to town and was so tired I couldn't half write, so now I will try and write a better one.

It is a dark and gloomy day today. All the folks have gone away this afternoon and I feel lonesome. I wish you were here to keep me company. I couldn't ask for anything better.

I would pay my large debt I owe — unless you would charge me too much, yes, you are quite a heartless creditor — Ha! Ha! Oh no, dear, I don't think you would take any more than what was coming to you.

I got a book about character today. It says you should marry someone born in September, but mine doesn't say I should marry one born in May. So I guess you will get along with me alright, but I won't with you, will I?

Of course, my dear, I think you will suit me fine, but according to your book, I will need my big candy knife to defend myself when you get angry at me, won't I? Ha. Ha.

Well, I don't have much faith in these character readings. If we seek to make each other happy, we will be happy. I shall always try to do that myself, and I believe you will, too.

Well, Edwin, I am willing to wait until spring to go home if I can take you along. I realize it takes lots of money to get married and get started and I know I would not be able to get married for several months if you were not going to help me out.

It will take about $50.00 to get ready and I will only earn $20.00 outside my room and board. I am trying to live as reasonably as I can, but I have been sick so much this summer and fall it has put me back.

I got a letter saying that my San bill is $15 and that does not include the treatments I am taking now. Maybe I can get them to wait a couple of months for it seeing we need so much money now. I guess they'll take it when they can get it anyway.

So, you were sick too, well I am glad you are better. If I had been there, I would have given you some good San treatments—they would have done you good. Well, I wish you were here to go downtown with me.

I'll bid you goodbye—with love,

Write right away,

Estella

Dec. 7, 1909
Grand Rapids, Mich.

Estella My Dear Little Girl,

Well, I guess you are not the only one to get a letter from their sweetheart, for I have just got one from mine, too, and I just want you to know that my sweetheart is just as nice as yours anytime, so there, you need not think your sweetheart is the whole thing for I think just as much of my own as you do of yours. Now!

I guess I had better stop before we really get to quarreling as to who is really the best, but I won't give up because mine is the best.

Yes, Stella, your letter came yesterday, but as usual, last night was my night at the armory. By the time I got supper for the company, it was after 12 o'clock when I got home. Ma was sitting up waiting for me. She said she hoped Estella would not have this to contend with very long. And I don't think you will--my enlistment will be out in another year, then I think I will be through with the National Guard. I will have another place to turn my attention. Then I will have my girl with me, and no need for any outside attractions. My place will be at home with her.

No, Stella dear, regardless of what my character reading may say, if you never have to use your candy knife until you have to defend yourself from me, it will remain a very, very long time untouched. I think the only time you would have to use it would be to prevent me from collecting those payments and I think perhaps you would have to use it quite freely then if you took a notion not to deliver those payments.

We are having our first real winter weather since we came back from Indiana. It has snowed all day and is quite cold tonight. I am really glad to see the snow if it would only stay for a little while. I think it is healthier than open winter weather, but these cold winters make me feel like I would like to go to Southern California or some other warm climate.

I am glad you have decided to wait until spring to go to Indiana, for I want very much to go with you and see my new Pa and Ma.

I am feeling better than I did, although I am not quite myself yet. I wish you were here to give me some of the San treatments you speak of, for I think they would help me.

I got the card with the funny address on it. It was some time before I could understand it until I saw your brother's name on it.

You said you were going to quit your work by Christmas. If you do that Stella, can you come up here sooner and stay until after New Year's? There are so many things I want to talk over and have you help me plan — please do this if you can, dear.

Now excuse this short and poorly written letter, for I am awful sleepy so I will say

Good night (with a kiss)

Write quick,

From your Edwin

P.S. Will send you some money on Friday.

A Clandestine Party

Dec. 20, 1909
Battle Creek, Mich.

My dear Edwin,

I have not heard from you yet, but I am guessing you reached home alright, I hope so anyway.

I am feeling stronger than when you were here, but I have a cold in my head that does not make me feel very good. How are you feeling by this time, dear?

I have been doing a lot of thinking since you were here and I have come to one conclusion at last. I have decided to tell you if it is alright with you, it will be a go.

Now Edwin, I ordered me a dress, but it is not made, and I can't have it done by Thursday. Under these circumstances, I think the best way is for me to get ready, pack up my things, and when I come Thursday, come to stay.

However, I don't want to do that unless we have the ceremony performed as soon as I get there on Thursday evening. Mama thinks that would be best too. She thinks you are alright.

I'm glad my folks like you real well for what they know of you. Do you wonder why I love you dear? I overheard Joe and Edith saying something about me liking you and Joe said, "Well I don't blame her, I like him too!" Ha! Ha!

Mama says I shouldn't keep you guessing all the time. She says I am mean to you, so I will have to be good if Mama says so, won't I?

I would like to have my dress done, but I can't, and I guess there are other things of more consequence than a dress. So if it is alright with you, I will come prepared for Thursday evening, the 23rd and we will have as simple an affair as possible.

I would rather just go to a minister's house or if you don't want to do that, you can have the minister come to your house. Don't tell anyone. Only your folks — and the fewer the better, for I won't be dressed for a wedding, and you know my feelings about the dress. So don't embarrass me with a crowd, will you sweetheart?

Now what shall I do about my bookcase and things? If I have money enough I can send them now, or send them COD or come back after New Year's and get them. Now, all these are suggestions; you write and let me know what to do. Do you want me to buy that candy and bring it when I come?

I will come on the same train you went on. Write right away, so I'll know what to do in time.

Lovingly,

Estella

P. S. I will send this by registered letter so if you get it right away, I will know your opinion before I come. If you register the letter, I can get it by Wednesday night or Thursday morning.

Epilogue

So dear reader, that was the last of the letters and if we did not know those who grew up with Edwin and Estella, we might wonder about their future, but there are close to thirty people alive today who owe their existence to that misplaced letter.

Edwin and Estella's wedding date was Dec 23, 1909.

Nearly one year later, Edwin's fears of being the last of his line would disappear because they would have a son born on Dec. 6, 1910 and name him Donald.

Donald was my grandfather and he was as much of a gentleman as you ever met. He was hardworking, honest, kind and gracious just like his parents — certainly a character worth having.

Donald was followed by his two sisters named Vivian and Lillian, who went by the nicknames of Dolly and Babe respectively. Despite Estella's dread of nicknames, she married a man who gave his sisters nicknames, and gave his daughters nicknames, so apparently she chose to pick her battles and let the nicknames slide.

Donald married Veronica Mellish and had two daughters — Elaine and Kathleen. They lost a son at birth — the greatest heartbreak of their lives.

Donald might have been the last of the line, but he loved his girls as much as if they were sons. And while the Ellis name was not carried on, the values of the White and Ellis families still run in our veins.

Edwin and Estella lived through some of the hardest times in America. They soon saw World War I, survived the depression and finally witnessed the stories unfolding of World War II. They relied on their faith in God to make it through those hard times. When Donald was eleven, Edwin joined Estella as a member of the Seventh-day Adventist Church.

Edwin finally got his dream of living in a warm place. During the depression, their son Don (who was an adult by then) went west to find a job in Southern California and Edwin and Estella soon joined him and his family.

Edwin wrote several marches. The most famous were "Flashlight" and "Napoleon's Last Charge."

Their home was filled with love, music and laughter. Their grandchildren remember it as a safe and warm place.

Edwin died in Paradise Valley, California in 1946. Estella lived on loving her children, grandchildren and great grandchildren until she died in Medford, Oregon in 1976.

I first remember meeting Estella when I was two and a half and she made me feel like the most important baby in the world. Throughout my childhood if I was in trouble with my Grandma, I could always count on Grammy Estella's room for a safe haven. She had a way of making her grandchildren and great grandchildren feel special. I cherish the memory of her smile.

Their descendants look forward to that great reunion where we can meet again and laugh over these letters, which in a way, have sent us a message from over a century ago and given us an example of how to love each other well.

Thank you, Edwin and Estella,
for your story and example of kindness and love.

Edwin and Estella on their wedding day, December 23, 1909

Love is patient,
Love is kind.
It does not envy,
It does not boast,
It is not proud.
It does not dishonor others,
It is not self-seeking,
It is not easily angered,
It keeps no record of wrongs.
Love does not delight in evil,
But rejoices with the truth.
It always protects, always trusts,
Always hopes,
Always perseveres.
Love never fails.

-1 Corinthians 13:4-8, NIV

You can visit Edwin and Estella's world
at Love Letters 1909 on Pinterest at
http://www.pinterest.com/flowerpower7/love-letters-1909/

You can listen to one of Edwin's marches on YouTube here
https://www.youtube.com/watch?v=V-ouf7J6F5Y

If you enjoyed this book,
please consider leaving a review on Amazon.com
so others can discover these letters of history and love.

www.ingramcontent.com/pod-product-compliance
Lightning Source LLC
Chambersburg PA
CBHW070812050426
42452CB00011B/2015